Roy Masters

THE ADAM AND EVE *SINDROME*

Edited by Robin Stevens

Foundation of Human Understanding
Los Angeles; Grants Pass, Oregon

Published by The Foundation of Human Understanding
Printed in the United States of America

For information, address
The Foundation of Human Understanding
P.O. Box 34036, 8780 Venice Boulevard
Los Angeles, California 90034

or

P.O. Box 811, 111 N.E. Evelyn Street
Grants Pass, Oregon 97526

Library of Congress Catalog Card Number: 85-80750

ISBN 0-933900-11-2

To my wife, Ann, and
all my kids—David, Dianne,
Michael, Alan, and Mark

*The palaces of kings
are built upon the
ruins of Paradise*

—*Thomas Paine*

Contents

Preface

There is a special reason why I do not write here about natural love; rather, I expose the seductive, unnatural, deceptive "love" for what it is, in order to dispel its manipulative power. Reading this, you might feel disturbed, personally threatened. You may even think, *this man is crazy!* If this happens, there can be only two explanations: either *I am* mad, or my revelations have touched a raw nerve.

Most of us take special pride in our sensitivities, our compassion, our needs and great capacity for love. Now along I come, saying all that is weakness, foolishness—worse—downright dangerous! Human love as we know it and as handed down to us is the root of all human misery! Here I claim that our attractions and needs are, in reality, blind compulsions, the aftereffects of some distant trauma. Like moths to the flame, we are drawn into the intricate seductions of hell; and out of that, we evolve those enslaving, debilitating, and agonizing thoughts and passions which at first blush we *think* of as love.

The disturbing disclosures in this work may cause you to deny or misconstrue what I am trying to say, to judge me as the supreme put-down artist. But I say that in order to reveal the truth, it is necesary to poke holes in the sacred cows of established—but false—beliefs.

Therefore, in this work I do not tell you what love or truth *is*, as much as expose what it is not. My purpose is to lead you beyond the painful realization of what a fool for "love" you have been. Thus forearmed, you can shrink from the next mistake you are poised to make and go on to experience the true fulfillment you are seeking.

Special thanks to the Courtauld Institute Galleries, London, for permission to use on our cover Lucas Cranach the Elder's *Adam and Eve* from their Lee Collection.

CHAPTER 1

The Adam and Eve *Sin*drome

An ancient flaw in her nature draws a woman to a weak man. This flaw teaches her to feel secure by making him fail. It also excites the weakness of the man to cling to her, which is what fuels in her a false sense of security, of power.

This mysterious flaw in woman's nature arises from the spirit of Original Sin; and its current mystique inherently and always appeals to, and supports, the compatible wrong in man. This misguided female spirit feels power through agreeing with what has gone wrong in man. To satisfy the need of this spirit, a man's ego must be stroked and gratified, progressively weakened, and eventually destroyed to keep her *happy*. But *happiness* is always short-lived, because she becomes possessed by a madness she can neither understand nor control.

Every woman instinctively inherits this *black widow spider* knowledge—tempting her man and sucking out his life juices. Men sense the danger, but they are drawn to fulfill the mysterious and original promise of a life of glory implicit in a woman's love. To get a man, *every* woman knows she must put him up on a pedestal. She rationalizes that selfish compulsion as her loving duty. It is not.

Man is also insecure. He inherits the guilt of a wounded pride, which is forever trying to recover by employing the original spirit of its fall—the woman—obligating her spirit to give what she really cannot deliver. It is as though his need were trying to draw up through her a spirit to make good its ancient promise. Instead of improving his lot with her affections, he is made progressively worse. As long as she continues to lie, offering herself like a Las Vegas dealer, he goes on hoping upon hope on the next turn of the dice. But he goes on losing, reinforcing the spirit of the *house* with his vital substance.

The very qualities that can produce real love, security, and happiness (such as good character and other noble moral traits) are the qualities which oppose lust. The lovesick female spirit can flourish only on excitement emanating from the worshipful clinging of a failing, egotistical man. It is threatened by real strength and virtue. While she needs this virtue in a man, her sick, egotistical spirit is afraid of being dominated by it.

A man of good character is not drawn to female guile, having little use for the appeal it has for other men. A guileful female has little use for this kind of man, because she knows she cannot have her way with him. If she wants to control a man, a woman must be of easy virtue, quick to recognize a man's ego *worth*. The favor of her body completes this slavery to her spirit.

Instant recognition of man's ego is the theme of the original lie, which has always stimulated the evolution of male flesh to rise at each falling away of the soul. Sex happens to be the original symptom of man's failing. It represents death coming alive, a new body replacing the dying one through the sin of pride. For man, death comes through sin, and that sin is pride.

2

The pride of man lives now amid the evolutions of sensuous *life* that arise through failing. The life of the flesh thus appears through the mechanism of Original Sin and again when we are sustained in our pride. The guilt of the soul is assuaged by identifying with the flesh. Prideful man is proud in his body when he is in love, prouder still when gratifying his evolving lusts. By viewing a man's sexual weakness as a virtue, a woman can, in effect, reinforce the pride of Original Sin with her body, keeping him caught up in her spell in the ecstasy of his failing. She drinks in his life substance like Dracula. While he revels in the illusive ecstasy of the lie, she assimilates his life substance.

The slightest hint of female acceptance produces the failing that is felt as lust. Relieving this lust is where a woman's *false* sense of worth, of loving duty, of security is fiendishly gratified. A woman worships to the end that *she might be worshiped*. In the egotistical sense, pleasing a man is her selfish way of pleasing herself. With no life of her own, she feels what she stimulates a man to feel.

To serve an ego is to weaken it to need service, so that in the end the one doing the serving is served, becoming an almost godlike source of both need and satisfaction of need. If man were *doing business* with God, there would be nothing wrong with this arrangement, because man would benefit, in the flesh, from His spirit.

But Satan's spirit (operating through female guile), having no life or power of its own, can reverse the divine order of things. Through the pride of the woman, Satan compels man to give up his life and makes himself the godlike ground of man's being by deceiving him about the purpose of his existence. There are certain types of

3

men who love to be sustained by deception, as well as women who love to deceive—then, again, there are those who do not.

Worship the ego, inspire the ego to become god, and that triggers failing. Stroke that failing when it appears, relieve the tension, and spiritual, as well as physical, life is drained away. Now begin again before man has time to see what is really going on.

The sick female spirit can never really be fulfilled through such false devotion. She is frustrated, because the quality of this love *is his very life*. It is not love at all. Too much sex feeds her demon spirit, but too little, threatens it. One moment she *just loves* his failing, and the next she hates his guts for it; yet from hating sex love rises a need for sex love to soothe her guilt.

Every woman's real happiness depends upon a man understanding her need for real love rather than sexual love. As long as a woman is guileful, she will suffer the agonies of (sexually) drawing spinelessly weak or violently weak men to her. Like it or not, every woman inherits some of the guile that appeals to, and excites, the ancient weakness of man; and that is what every man must eventually come to grips with. The more guile she possesses, the more exciting is the woman. The greater her guile, the greater is her capacity to *fill up* on weak men.

It must be understood here that people are capable of both wholesome and unwholesome needs and desires. I am speaking now only of unwholesome desires. The lower nature must be overcome, or else it consumes the higher one, which is waiting to unfold. Sin (or guile), when it enters the soul, supplants a holy love that a man

4

and woman might have for one another. Corruption replaces natural desires with a terribly destructive hunger for one another. *Deep down what a woman really wants is to be loved for herself, not for her body* or for the resident hell that men selfishly embrace for the sake of the continuance of their pride.

The pride of man, as it has originated through its woman-mother, needs mothering to survive. It has little use for sobering goodness, simply because honesty does not help pride to survive; it does not light the evolutionary and imaginary fires of mind and body. Innocence is not the stuff that dreams (and false confidence) are made of. Deceit excites imagination, but honesty threatens to awaken the prideful spirit to its death.

As I have already pointed out, our mortal nature has come down to us from an original ego falling-away from an inner ground of being. The pride in its sensuous form is nurtured by the betraying spirit of its original conversion. Man's confidence (belief in himself) has been altered from what it might otherwise be, founded on his faith in a God greater than himself. Because he is wrong, he needs a woman to believe in him in order to go on believing in himself and his prideful way. Man's soul is adapted psychologically and spiritually to depend on a woman's pretentious affection. His insanity craves and demands support from the ancient wrong in women. His "courage" to continue in the prideful way comes through a lying love. From lying love comes the motivation to be more of a beast, doing wrong things and living the wrong way without guilt. But afterward the guilt appears.

By reason of his sin a man is addicted to a woman's love but afraid of what it does to him. True courage springs from being right. No one can stand alone or be certain when he is wrong unless he has some kind of reassurance; that is why all insecure, weak men need a woman's love. The comforter of the wrong man is his god.

Pride has little tolerance for innocence. Innocence sees through error and does not support it. When, through ambition, selfishness, anger, and greed, a man loses his virtue and *true* courage, then in his failing, he looks for the *false* to sustain him. Then there ceases to be in him the spirit of true adventure that the good Lord intended. He seeks, instead, for a different kind of confidence for a different way—for those forbidden things of power and glory. From *wine, women, and song* he gets the false courage to go out into the world and fight, cheat, and wrestle the goods and glory from other men. Each man, backed by his woman's love, becomes a bigger beast instead of a better man.

Each man, guilty from his encounters with other beasts, comes home to his woman, obligating her to remind him that he *is* a man and help him forget his failing and what he has become. Renewing his confidence sexually, she sets him up to fail again and again. Debilitated, afraid to work and compete, he begins to spend time with the ego reinforcements of sex, booze, and drugs.

Winners and losers in the dog-eat-dog world of pride both become less, not more. The filthy rich have their women to soothe away the hurt of playing the rejection game and so do the downtrodden. Pride is such a scoundrel that it is able to use not only the weakness of sexual love, but also its eventual failing, to sustain itself. Pride can hide behind any weakness, even impotence, and make it seem like a virtue.

When a man sets a woman up to accept him, he is really making her, rather than himself, into a god. She is a god who learns to feel secure only through the power drawn from his sexual abuse of her, for which reason she allows this abuse. Once she becomes addicted to his clinging, she becomes bossy and demanding. Now he begins to fail not only out there in the world, but also at home in bed as well. Here, in ego desperation, he may turn to other women or teach his wife to degrade herself to excite him to fail. Only in failing can he experience the awakening of new sexual feelings, which evolve out of the sin of man's soul as it reaches new lows of depravity.

From the love tease he now falls to the hate tease. He wallows in blame, resentment, and hate. He is fixated to that just as much as he was to love, because blaming her is also a powerful distraction from guilt. However, because hate is a response to her temptation and is itself a sin, it produces a new "life" feeling of sexual lust that, when milked for relief, produces only waves of anguish and guilt in the man. This conflict, when relieved through blame or violence, turns to lust again, and so on, endlessly; finally someone is hurt or killed.

It is man's need, the implanted sin, that tempts woman to tempt him. He rubs her as if to get the genie out of the bottle! Without God's grace to help her withstand a man's sexual pressure, a woman is tempted to relieve the pressure through sexual service. If her behavior does not rise out of guile, then it rises out of the guilt of resenting his pressure. Relieving a man's sexual demands is her way of controlling his rage and smothering her own resentment with his failing love.

He pressures, she resents him, she fears him, she descends into guilt, which she tries to relieve by yielding to

7

his demands. But he is not better off. He feels cheated and resents her as if it were all her fault. Sex, in becoming a way of controlling a man's rage, also becomes the key to controlling and degrading the man himself. But sexual service cannot really diminish her own private guilt. On the contrary, it is increased. The man is angry again, she is upset again. She feels resentment, which becomes guilt.

Her guilt makes the woman feel responsible for the man's misery, and so she relieves it to relieve her own—and everything gets worse. Her amorous consideration does nothing except teach a man to be angry in order to have his way. Suppose she stops giving him sex. Then he may grow violent again or beg—that, too, will make a woman feel guilty. But if she obliges him, he will become *more* violent or craven next time. And so it goes. Whether he gets sex or not, he hates her and blames her.

While it is *really all his fault*, his pride refuses to see that fact. His pride must be forever served by the evil of her love and by his hatred of her deceit. If he feels guilty for his own violence, he then becomes a pathetic puppy, begging for reassuring sex, changing the rage a woman feels into pity, which becomes translated into sexual sympathy toward her subject. By giving sexual love, she tries to soothe her own guilt, doing her inherited duty for his failing pride.

Deep inside her private hell the ancient Serpent saps life energy from the woman's soul. She, in turn, drains it from the man. Ever since the dawn of history in the Garden of Eden, *man has loved woman only for the teasing thing that lives within her* and rarely for the woman herself. Poor, misguided fool! He can only reward her failing with his own, for sex is the only love he knows how to give.

8

While there are many dyed-in-the-wool whores who revel in getting away with this sort of murder, there are also many sincere women who cannot find pleasure in it. The contempt of a decent woman is different from her sinister sister's in that her soul cannot find pleasure in being a destroyer. She simply cannot enjoy the false security of sexual power. Her sincerity allows her to see the folly of it all. Her contempt consists mostly of resenting men for their inability to save her from the indwelling evil that comes with such power.

Real women have no ambition for power, and so they suffer from the power that they inherit simply from being female. Unfortunately, their resentment locks them into their mate just the way it does with other women.

The physical sensitivity to women, while it is the very thing men need to reinforce their egos, is actually the source of their downfall. And blaming women for it is the other side of their downfall! Blame is an emotion of escape. Like the "love" that precedes it, it provides a false innocence—a protection from shame. It is this violent failing that awakens the love monster of sensuality, a monster doomed to be further degraded by its own resentment and blame, which generate greater lust, until the woman is no more—perhaps murdered.

The reassuring love that man demands causes conflict in both the woman and himself, and between them. Her hatred of him leads her (through guilt) to lose herself in his love. When this *love* is seen for what it is (betrayal and wickedness), they come to hate one another and are driven to distraction, violence, heart attacks, diseases, strokes, and many illnesses. In the absence of understanding, the sex impulse is never resolved and degenerates into a dangerous thing.

9

No matter what the problem is, if you can't understand it, you can't solve it. Without realizing what is happening, man falls in love with the principle of his own destruction. People despise politicians, yet they elect them. The reason for this is that the collective ego of man has become a friend of the lie and a lover of liars. It is that evil which men embrace when it lies to them and employ again when they resent its injustice. Both love and hate feed the vicious, slimy, sneaky pride of man.

Beginning with a woman, a man's entire existence revolves around embracing one form of evil or another. Through the trauma of any sin, the death self enters the mind and tortures you until you sin again. Identifying with this indwelling evil, you feel what it feels, even the guilt it suffers in the light of reality. The pain comes from evil's conflict with the purifying inner light, but because you identify with the evil, its resentment toward correction is felt as your very own. This is the rejection of God, which makes the pain so unbearable that it forces you to escape into the pleasures of sin, where sin upon sin enlarges sin itself—a woman in her way and a man in his.

The woman's inflamed soul, tortured by the need for power, is forced to fill itself again and again by teasing a man to death. So involved is he in the evolution of his ego through the hypnosis of this intrigue that he cannot find the truth which would save them both.

Evil thoughts arrange themselves in such a way that they always make you doubt the truth. A woman is deceived in her mind when she believes she must save a man or make him over with her love. The satisfaction she feels in trying to prove herself is the strength of the failing man, draining away to feed her private demon. Her *strength* is his strength. Her false security is based on deception—lying to him, lying with him.

The fact that her great love has actually created a Frankenstein monster or a pathetic wretch becomes a truth she cannot handle, for a woman's love is supposed to be a glorious thing, the creation of man in the reflection of her greatness. Instead, her love is seen for what it is. Shouldn't her experience demonstrate to her that there is something terribly wrong with woman's love? For the most part it does not.

A woman resents her own failing and will try harder to prove her goodness. The more sex is promoted, the more unreasonable she will become, and the more the man will react unreasonably to her. Until the day he is willing to face himself and give up his pride, the man will go mad with violent frustration or *bleed* to death through sex and secret rage. He will die from blaming the woman for what is wrong due to his own failing in life rather than face up to his responsibility. After all, isn't that the nature of pride? In its wrong it will never admit it is wrong, and that is why men need women who agree with their wrong: and women only agree with it for power.

If a woman *loves* sex, it is only because she has exchanged roles with the man or confused sex with love. She will demand sex more and more and more, until her husband becomes impotent and her security is threatened. If she becomes too terrified to yield to her husband's sexual demands, it is because she is aware of the demon inside her, gaining power over them both.

If a man also becomes terrified of his wife's demands, it is because he associates sex with the love that he taught her to want from him. When he comes to the end of his capacity to satisfy her growing need, he is forced to realize his inadequacy through the evidence of his impotence. Because the woman's security is based on his weakness, she feels betrayed by his failure. Without the power of his weakness to make her feel secure, she is threatened. Dependent on sex love, a woman fears rejection.

What a dilemma the poor woman is in! She can revel in the pleasure of contempt for his sexual abuses of her, encouraging them for the ecstasy of judgment. With sex she becomes guilty. Without it she discovers the guilt. The very thing she craves to make her secure makes her more insecure. Her loathing produces a need for loving, and loving, a need for loathing.

A woman who is conditioned to accept the idea that sex is love will always be frustrated. Her sick soul encourages abuse for her own gratification. *She uses his use.* Drunk on the wine of sexual power, she loses sight of her real insecurity and of how ugly both she and her husband have become.

To resolve this "Adam and Eve" *sin*drome, one must first succeed in meditation. Freed from the seductive forces of the imagination, one finds the inner strength to build a new existence around a spiritual center rather than around the ruination of one's fellows. The palaces of kings are built on the ruins of Paradise. The sensuous ego life has Satan's nature at its core. For he has known from the beginning how his kingdom was to come. Being without power himself, he must steal it by deception. That tragedy which began in Paradise repeats itself endlessly, projecting its horror into descending generations.

The lesson to be learned here should be clear by now. Man is an *unnaturally* natural creature. Pride in sensuality is simply *pride in a failing*. Without knowing how she knows it, the guileful female understands this fact. She rises to cater to a man's weakness in order to establish her power, which in the light of reality is seen to be Satan's power over both her *and* her man. From her, through him, come all the horrors and tragedies of this life.

Therefore, dear ladies, if you really want to help your husband, if you *truly* love your man and wish him to live long, then DISCOURAGE his amorous advances; but be careful not to reject him (there is a difference). Gentlemen, if you really love your wife, then be good enough to overcome your selfish, craven need to use her for all she's worth. Wrestle with yourself for her sake, and she will recognize that struggle, and your diminishing use of her body, as real love for her. Soon a strange thing will begin to occur. You will have less sex but you will enjoy it more. It will be more enjoyable because love is involved with failing less.

If a man gets what his ego needs from lying with a woman, it comes across as *using her*. She feels the love and hate of it, the endless cycle of frustration and hopeless despair. But lying together when using her *less* (and failing less) comes across as love, because instead of taking advantage of her exciting body, he denies his own selfish need out of consideration for her real need. Now she can draw upon his divine love to save him from her, and her from her private torment.

If you are using, you cannot be loving. No one can use and love another at the same time. The rule is use less, love more; use more, love less: because if you are not using, then you *are* loving.

13

Marriage was never meant to be an institution within which men might freely abuse their women or women use men's use of them. For in this deadly ego game women rise like devils from a pit, and men live forever in rebellious, sickly submission. And both live in terror. Marriage is a holy framework, ordained by our Creator, within which man can, in the expression of his weakness, come one day to understand and transcend it.

If marriage fails, it is because there is error in people, not in the institution of marriage. Marriage is not wrong, people are! Yet marriage is blamed. It is meant to help men learn to fail less and, with God's love, to rise above the carnal nature. Sex outside marriage can never be anything but mutual use. The grace to overcome the carnal nature can be found only within a framework of honor, where the Father meant it to be found. There can be only use in fornication, and through it man is condemned to death.

Marriage is the place where man can, if he will, lead the woman out of the female, and the female out of her private hell. Here is where Adam finally says "Put the apple down, Eve. I don't want to support my pride anymore; I just want to do right by you." At first your Eve may think you're crazy; she may feel threatened and try to confuse you, but something inside her, in the midst of much protesting, will breathe a sigh of relief.

CHAPTER 2

What's a Woman to Do?

A decent woman doesn't mind joining her body to her husband as long as he is an honorable man. For a woman, sex is an unspoken agreement with whatever her man is. If he is considerate, virtuous, thoughtful, a good money manager, and a strong, responsible father, then there is value in the relationship. But if her man is thoughtless, selfish, reckless, and lustful, a woman is bound to bring out any hidden despicable qualities through her sexual ego support.

A man's deteriorating condition is what makes his wife's future seem so bleak. It threatens her and makes her afraid of sex. Sex is his problem; what to *do* with his problem is hers. (While I acknowledge that there are certain types of women who enjoy the leverage they have with weak and criminal types, I am not dealing with them in this text.)

It is good to agree with a good man and dangerous to support a weak or bad one. No harm is ever done cooperating with goodness, be it in president or husband. On the contrary, there is great benefit to be derived, for that is the basis of true love and heaven's kingdom on earth.

Alas, it is not possible to go along with a lustful, ambitious, or selfish man without suffering terrible consequences. Certainly, dirty old men need love too, but when you give it to them, they only become more filthy. What's a woman to do?

She has a duty to her husband, of course, but how can a decent woman perform that duty when she awakens to realize the kind of a man she's married? Can you see why the sexual problems that men and women have with one another are not so much a matter of sex as a matter of principle or lack of it?

The decent woman's dilemma always revolves around a weakness in a man. His fault makes her give him a hard time. He has only himself to blame in losing his self-respect. She finds herself losing her desire to cohabit.

Sex may indeed be a woman's duty, but it is only the duty of a right-minded female toward a right-minded male.

We all get married with dumb, romantic notions uppermost in our minds, but the pain of our wrong motives should eventually awaken us to the awareness of their presence and their meaning. When the woman awakens before the man to find herself whorishly serving the selfish need of an unspiritual beast, with nothing but a dead end for a future, it is only natural for her to have fears and second thoughts about her destiny with him.

Here is where a bright-minded woman can easily slip into confusion through her own eagerness to be right. The Bible bids a woman to submit to her husband, and a hypocritical "Christian" husband is usually quick to ram that fact down her throat. The private serpent coiled up inside every woman may seize upon such thoughts and

16

cause the woman to doubt herself. These thoughts may also serve a wicked woman, who is so ambitious that she will herself hide her real motive behind a pretended sense of duty, continuing to use and manipulate a man's use of her and calling it love.

A woman can make sex seem God-inspired, a sacrifice she makes to *keep the family together*, when in reality it is nothing but a selfish power trip. Because she is the source of what a fallen man has come down to be, happiness—that is, her own ego idea of her own goodness—will depend upon giving her *creation* the *divine support* he was *created* to cry for. He needs her, and out of her great love and exalted sense of duty, she satisfies his need. To the pride of a woman, variations on this argument are natural to believe and difficult to resist.

The best chance that a potentially decent man has to see the light is for his woman (his god) to awaken him to see his selfish use of her. How can she do this? By *lovingly refraining* from her selfish *duty* instead of performing it.

Long ago God gave Adam a woman to love, but he used her instead. The human race has had to pay a bitter price for his mistake, and it is still paying.

I have often admonished my son about his selfishness toward his mother and father. I have pointed out the twenty years I have clothed, fed, and watched over him, and yet how hard it is for him to extend a few thoughtful courtesies, such as washing a few dishes or taking out the garbage without being told! But he will go to the moon and back for his girlfriend's smile. Everyone gets what is coming to them . . .

Good parents are to their children as God was to Adam. A girlfriend will love a man for his selfish ambition, though neither God nor his parents will. His wrong comes alive in the presence of her wrong, but it is only the selfishness of a woman that can agree with the selfishness of a man. For her agreement he will end up cultivating the demon in her that he should have corrected. Had he loved his parents and become acquainted with their goodness, he would have known how to love and correct a woman, as he was loved.

Beginning with his girlfriend, he does a lot of "good" for all the wrong people in his life, good that rewards the wrong in them in exchange for serving his ego. Everyone takes advantage. He loses everything and gains nothing. And what does his woman get instead of love? She gets useless material things and disgusting sex—nothing that truly satisfies.

Once set firmly on this path, he is doomed to spend his substance giving to all the wrong people. They will play along, pretending love and respect in order to take every possible advantage. And it jolly well serves him right! When the love of God is not paramount in a man's heart, he must unwittingly employ the devil *her*self to support him in his selfish way of life. The more guilty he is, the more he needs and uses *it* in her, drawing hell up through her to make their lives bitter.

Which is the greater love, for a bartender to give his customer a drink with sympathy or to withhold it, giving a sobering "shot" of truth, instead? Surely you can see that it is more loving to withhold the drink of comfort and to sober the drunk with truth. But to be able to withhold sympathy or booze, *one must be secure in oneself and, therefore, unselfish.* Just how many female "bartenders" who have built their existence around serving can afford

18

to be that unselfish? Without hope of a better way, such unselfishness seems certain self-destruction.

If you can recognize the *real* duties of the bartender, then apply the same principle to your own situation. It's true that your *customer* may go and find some other *joint* with a *bartender* who has more sympathy for his sick ego need, but this female will surely be another who takes advantage, and not a real friend.

If there really were a bartender who told the truth and withheld lying comfort, he would certainly lose the security of his bar world with all its sick inhabitants. Yet, on the other side of that experience, he just might find an appreciative friend.

It is hard to speak the truth to lovers, husbands, and friends, because our selfish pride has built its existence on catering to theirs. We feel a false sense of responsibility toward others that is selfish in nature; our obligations toward them are motivated only to preserve their value to us.

As a woman, you must abandon your present perverted duties, which only preserve a selfish, but self-defeating, security around the principle of deception. One way or another, once you have taken that terrifying first step, you will most certainly find a different life, perhaps with a friend you never knew you had. The worst thing that could happen is that you could find yourself alone, starting life all over again—minus the presence of the beast you should never have been joined to had you been right, in the first place. Just how much you *lose* depends on how *well* you have played the game in the past and how far you have traveled down that path.

As a woman, you have built your life around a "drunk." When you awaken to what you are doing to him and what he, in turn, is doing to you—to the kind of *living* you are making off of his weakness—you will see that there is no future in serving him that way. Caution, please! Don't ever be bitter. Look, instead, at the kind of woman you were that was attracted to this kind of man. Were you *really* doing your duty for this drunken, contemptible, impossible creature? As a *born-again* woman, surely you can see no real future, no love or honor in that arrangement.

Now you find yourself married to a man but somehow divorced from him in spirit. Something more has to change. You have come from a marriage made in hell, which, if you have the fortitude and fidelity to see it through to the end, can become a marriage made in heaven. At worst your barroom bum will desert you, in which case his infidelity *frees* you from an unwholesome bond that should never have existed. But if he should awaken to see your *real* love, then you will have yourself a real man.

The very moment you meet someone determines the future course of events for good or for evil. The future is building through *every* present moment, depending on what your secret motive is.

Brides, carefully consider the man you are to marry, bearing in mind that you will be responsible for amplifying all his faults, hidden or obvious. Guilt will grow from this kind of love. For goodness' sake, steer clear of a man who drinks, smokes, takes drugs, or is high on religion! It is only the wickedness in you that can be stirred to play God or to *make over* such an obviously weak creature.

Except on the ground of unfaithfulness, *never initiate divorce or be tricked into giving one;* let the other party bear the sin of it. Although you have the right to divorce an unfaithful man, it is better to separate and see if he changes.

Your heart must always bear goodwill and be true. Never use his or anyone else's wrong to excuse the wrong you want to do. Be loyal to the end, regardless of whether he is or not, so that by your perfect example he might be awakened to doubt *his* way and choose truth. How can he choose the right way when you are wrong? Your wrong tempts and provides the excuse for more wrong and revenge. But in the light of your fidelity, he can reflect upon his own conduct toward you. He perceives his own fault instead of yours.

Your gentle forbearance provides a choice he never had. Honor draws a boundary line and dares him to step across. If the right way does not exist in you, then the wrong way does, and that makes you guilty not only of failing but also of temptation. The ancient dilemma of choice remains: the devil and the deep blue sea, the frying pan and the fire.

How can you ever know the heart of a person unless you draw it to the surface with divine love? You owe it to your Creator to awaken others to goodness. If it's there in you, people will respond to it with hope.

Perfect goodwill is a mystery of faith. Its magic is able to touch the goodness in a soul and make it respond, unfolding in a special way. If goodwill is not there in you, the evil will is, causing others to stumble. Set aside resentment, and there is goodwill. Bearing goodwill, your conscience will be clear no matter what happens.

You owe only one thing; to repent for past sins and be true to what you know is right in your heart from now on.

Abandon resentment, hold fast and have faith in what you know. Reveal the light that shines beyond patience. Loving God means holding fast to what you are given to realize is right; that is your first duty. Not loving in the old way *is* loving in the new way.

Speaking truly is an unselfish thing. Honesty is what others need, even when it hurts. Honesty is unselfish because you know your old life depends on lies and *benefits* obtained by pretending to love.

The wrong your husband once embraced is the same wrong he blames when things go amiss. One moment you are loved for your wrong and the next you are hated. Now you must begin to pull that rug out from under his world of pride. If he must judge, let him judge you for what is right. Give him a chance to repent or to find another *cell mate* with whom to commit adultery and obtain ego support.

Even if he should set you free in this way, there is an extra reward awaiting you if you remain unattached. Wait now, and see if the pain of terrible experiences will awaken him to the error of his ways. (Believe me, in this period of waiting, you can learn much about yourself as well.)

It is a terrible thing for a person to wake up one morning and realize the tragic mistake he has made. How beautiful it would be to find you waiting, unmarried, faithful, and true! Can you not see how much greater love and respect there will be? And the guiding light within you will become the catalyst for restoring that faith and taking away all bitterness.

How terrible it is to awaken and find a part of you joined illicitly to someone else! Marry a divorced woman, and you can feel yourself married to her former husband. There he is inside her, mocking, standing between you and paradise. Marry a divorced man, and there, in him, is the other woman. It's bizarre, like a woman having sex with another woman—even a mother.

And how you will hate your new husband for tempting you to marry! You couldn't wait, and so rather than see your own weakness for his weakness, you blame him for failing you, for using you and taking advantage at a time when you were most vulnerable.

Here there can be no goodwill to touch the soul with its magic. Had that man known true love, he would not have been a *lover*; he would have guided you instead to wait and see if your mate would come around. A man like this you could have respected, for by his example you would have been restored to self-respect. Instead, you have a two-time loser who bears your two-timing contempt.

If you wait, you might discover that you have driven your husband to another woman because your clinging, your ego struggling to maintain a sense of security for yourself, was draining his life away. In your egotism and insecurity, in your unconscious desire to dominate, you were yourself demanding sick love from this man. In your blindness you continually set him up to fail, to fall sexually so that you might fulfill a sick need for judgment, perhaps set in motion long ago by your hatred of your father. You might also see how you weakened him through building his ego, inspiring him to go out and get what *you* wanted (the way your mother did with your father).

If you had waited yourself, sir, you might have discovered (for example) that your weakness had driven your own wife to seek in other men the love she could never get from you. But can the kind of man who offers that *love* be any better than you were to her? Surely he will confound her even more!

But if you had waited, contemplating your sin, she might have awakened to see her own. In waiting, there comes a change that your wife can sense. If the good is in you, the good in her will be drawn to it.

Through our wrong motives of ambition and selfishness, we make enemies into "friends" and friends into enemies. But if our intent is pure, all obstacles can be surmounted.

A pure intent opens the portals of the soul in such a way that only goodness can pass, but no evil can enter. A person with evil intent has this right door of his mind closed and the wrong one open.

It is an eerie experience living with a selfish person. Unbeknown to him, he has made himself a habitation for hell. Happily, all the designs of that vicious spirit will be frustrated if you will but hold fast to what you know is right and *never give ground.*

Therefore, be forever charitable, patient, and forgiving. Never allow the door of your mind to open through intimidation or seduction. Do not return evil for evil, but overcome evil with good.

CHAPTER 3 You Always Hurt the One You Lust

A person can lust for just about anything you care to think of, for lust replaces what was lost by love's failing.

A woman stands behind a man's ambition in order to fulfill her own. She may not soon feel the pain of this sin, so long as she reaps the rewards of her guile in terms of his lust and money.

A proud man lusts for the lying comfort that sustains his ambitions and soothes his soul. He becomes a slave for the sake of it. This is precisely the underlying problem between man and woman.

The human female form is no ordinary animal, for in that voluptuous *home* lurks the spirit of the original fall of man. For this reason alone man must approach a woman's threshold with caution.

The male sexual urge is not an ordinary animal desire either; it is subtly connected to an underlying ego need for the guile of a mother spirit. Man's need to be mothered betrays his fallen and misguided nature, always seeking its *creator*. When the companion spirit of woman rises to fulfill this need, a mysterious force sexually renews itself at the expense of the dying man. Great wisdom is needed to live and practice innocent sex (in an original fallen state) without falling further away and corrupting oneself with the dominant female will.

In all proper human relationships there are boundaries, protocols, and manners that are designed to protect us from trespassing on each other's privacy, human dignity, and rights. As a guest in someone else's home, you don't just walk over to the refrigerator and help yourself to refreshment. You wait upon the graciousness of your host. If you rudely step over that boundary, then that is the beginning of problems between the two of you. If he is wise, your host will not let you return, and that should end the relationship. If he lacks a strong sense of propriety and a strong character, your host may let you get away with your bad manners, in which case, the result of not being corrected will be to encourage you to go on taking liberties.

A weak, people-pleasing host, wanting to be liked, will be confounded by his own resentment, which he most likely conceals with false politeness. Incidentally, that show of friendship (intended to cover up inferiority, guilt, and weakness, which grow out of resentment itself) may be the reason you, as an intruder, will be encouraged to be even more ill-mannered and rude.

There is a protocol also that all men must observe in their relationships with women. A man cannot walk into a woman's "house" and make himself cozy without serious consequences; nor should any woman allow that. For those special privileges of intimacy, a man must be married—and married with a deep commitment to what is right in his heart. From this commitment springs a profound sense of honor and responsibility toward the woman.

There are many levels on the descent into hell. Traveling down through each level, one reaches the threshold of ever lower worlds that one is enticed to cross. The first boundary was crossed by Adam's partaking of the forbidden *fruit of glory*. As the result of this first misstep, man's nature was altered to become the male subject of the spirit of the female who was once a woman.

The second boundary is a *love*, or sexual, one. The third has to do with resentment-based judgments. Insofar as man has become a male animal, he will be possessed by a powerful sexual urge. If he is a reason-loving animal, he will ponder the meaning of the awkwardness of this urge and eventually perceive the truth behind it. *He will be most careful not to use sex as a means of reinforcing his ego.* Such understanding exists only where man senses that sex is a symptom of an original spiritual failure passed down to him.

However, the pride of man, being what it is, prefers to renew the pattern of Original Sin, rejecting the truth by regarding the sexual failing as a virtue to be worshiped. Such rebellious, callous souls have little regard for the boundaries of propriety. On the contrary, they *must* venture across to the forbidden.

Pride is compelled to sin, to disobey reason in order to renew a false sense of well-being. Alas, across those borders you will find not the glories you imagine, but a velvet hell.

Men degenerate and are controlled through the complex passions of lust and hate. So important is it for a man to feel the evolution of his pride, that he will cross over the forbidden line at the expense of his body and soul. So important is it for an ambitious woman to feel the false life of power, that she will literally tease a man to death for it. Now every time he joins his body in sin to hers, hell evolves between them. Under these conditions, people develop either an aversion or an addiction to each other's bodies. It is not unusual for a man's soul to feel so guilty for using a woman, yet so addicted to using her, that he marries her and ends up trapped by his own weakness. While he might show love and commitment on the surface, his addiction underneath is a seething mass of resentment. His guilt draws him sexually closer to, or further from, the woman.

Suppose it is the woman who develops an aversion first and withdraws her sexual support. If he does not find another body to satisfy his lust, he feels rejected and threatened and so begins to resent her. This resentment gives rise to lust, lust leads to her rejection, rejection leads to more resentment. Now it is the temptation of resentment all by itself that drains him of energy, creating many fears and phobias—very often zombie-victim diseases like asthma or leukemia.

In science it is often important to add one chemical to the other, rather than the other to the one; for even in lifeless chemistry there are rules that must be obeyed to prevent explosions.

Marriage is not simply a matter of joining bodies, but of joining spirits. Either the man joins himself to the woman, or the woman joins herself to the man. Joining himself to the woman in ignorance, a man falls into very serious trouble. The reason, again, is that man is an animal because of the original sin of pride. That is, he is a procreating beast, alleviating the anxiety of an inherited failing with the woman who caused it. The nature of this failing (sin) must be taken into account in every relationship with a "*loving*" woman.

If it is true that God gave woman to man to *love* if it is true that man failed to love woman and, instead, used her to support and justify the wrong of his unconscious ego quest for glory, if it is true that man tempted woman to tempt him, and if it is true that man lost his *bright human nature* and became a procreating animal, then we shall find the evidence of this in *all* men born of woman who leave their mothers and fathers, coming back full circle to the woman-mother of their fallen existence.

Now, if we are ever to stop descending and begin rising, we must understand what the problem between man and woman is—a mysterious, descending spiral down through lust and resentment (known as love and hate). You see, what appears to be love is really an addiction to an existence that originally evolved from, and presently revolves around, the female role of goddess worshiping *god's* failing. Man still uses woman to reinforce and to perfect the animal illusion of pride that lost them Paradise. Woman is still slyly using man's use of her; and God is forever making good His sentence of death for sin.

There was once an Original Sin of disobedience involving choice, but our disobedience is not a matter of choice anymore. It is one of compulsion, to make those little bits of death called *sex* seem like life.

Always and without fail, what begins with two lovers in an apparent paradise ends up with two beasts fighting in a jungle hell. Pity the poor children born into this environment. They grow up (if they are lucky) and leave their crazy mothers and fathers. Each goes out into the world imprinted with the same uncorrected, mad ego message, seeking a soul mate, only to find a "*cell mate*," repeating the ancient sin of ignorant forebears.

Prideful parents can't help but instill pride in their off-spring. The inherent failure of love produces, without fail, the evil, violent, and seductive animals we all become. Children develop this pride through a love-hate they feel toward their parents. They grow up insecure, seeking security for their troubled souls with the opposite sex in the classic way of error.

Once pride gets inside us, it becomes (in a sense) a child of the devil, seeking comfort from the female god who tempted it and caused it to exist. In order to keep a man "*happy*," a woman must sink ever lower to excite and feed this thing in him that wants her to be a whore rather than a real woman.

Perhaps you can see how important it is for a woman to join herself to an *honorable* man, a man of character, love, and understanding. Only by completing herself through agreement with the virtue in him can she hope to be saved from the legacy of her private hell. A wise woman diligently seeks the kind of man who can help her accomplish this marvelous goal. But how can this be if a man, still full of pride, is bent on using his woman to sustain all the selfish ambitions of his pride? How can he save her? How can he save himself from her? How can he love the hell *out* of her if he is loving the hell *in* her? The law is that *one always ends up being used by what one uses, dominated by the spirit (object) of the use.*

The male victim lusts after a sense of completion that comes only from hell, and a sense of freedom which is only *from* the truth of what a beast he is.

Therefore, wherever there is a man who is weak and needs mothering, who is egotistical and unable to stand alone to reach his goals, or who is unwilling to bear the shame of his vileness, violence, and guilt, there you will find a woman appointed to be his comforter and his god, unknowingly perpetuating all the evils of Original Sin. Joining himself to the woman in weakness, man remains the instrument of a female-based hell through his lust.

Since the beginning, woman has possessed the inherent power to deceive, to pretend to fulfill the ancient selfishness of pride. She reinforces the promise of glory made by the Serpent in Paradise. To the pride of man, the seductive, naughty spirit in her appears as an angel, waiting to usher him to his kingdom.

For this reason the sexes are always troubled when they come together in ignorance of their heritage. It is in ignorance that man joins himself to woman, rekindling the ancient contract with sin. He burns with unquenchable lust for life from the god-mother of all living.

One morning the bubble of illusion breaks. Man and woman wake up in a *paradise* changed into a hell on earth that they have perversely created for one another. He overtly or secretly blames the woman for his own weakness; she hates him for what he has become to her but mostly blames herself as creator.

Can you see why fornication is evil and why adultery is even worse? Marriage alone is the framework that God has ordained to enable the male and the female to resolve their problems of pride through sex. Only within the wholesome boundary of matrimony can there be found the leading of God's holy spirit of love to save man from woman and to save the woman from herself.

Man born of woman is not a real man. To become a real man, a husband must use his wife less to love her more. The trouble is that a selfish male is threatened by a real woman. He desecrates her innocence and draws up out of her sin a female bitch for his pleasure-taking. This bitch is in charge of the next generation.

Call upon God now in your hour of need to save you from the female hell. Our Creator will lead the man out of the male and, through the remolding of the man, lead the woman out of the female in hell. This kind of future, this kind of love and correction, is what every female wants without knowing *what it is she teases for*. But men embrace the tease instead of correcting it.

Only within the framework of matrimony can the resolving power of love exist. Any relationship outside of marriage can never, ever be anything but mutual abuse and tease—selfish men using women and selfish women gaining unholy power, using use.

Of course, marriage does not necessarily guarantee salvation. After all, people get married for a variety of selfish reasons. Marriage without honor and divine guidance, like adultery, is made in hell and destined for damnation.

The observation of such degeneracy from a child's point of view has given marriage a bad reputation—so much so that young people are tempted to avoid the *certain* hell of marriage by the *apparent* heaven of living together. But marriage itself is not at fault, it is the people! If republicanism fails and becomes a dictatorship, it is not due to the failing of the principles of republicanism but to the sick people who abuse the system.

Where a bond exists between man and his conscience, there also is loving authority over the female nature in the woman. This authority can correct the woman from her female role. The witch who gets her own way through sex fails to become a real woman with a real man. Refusing to correct it, the selfish man actually employs the temptation in her, using every opportunity to extract that illusive something which his stupid ego craves from female tease. Here is where sex degenerates to lust.

Innocent sex differs from lustful sex in the practice of self-control. With innocent sex there is no further development of pride, so man remains close to his original fallen state of being. Sex becomes lust only when the pride in man refuses to face up to what sex means in terms of failing. It begins to reject truth by escaping into sensuality as it rises with the help of a lying and worshipful partner.

Lust breeds failing and failing breeds lust. Lust is an addiction controlled by the hell in woman, willing and worming its way through the weakness of man's soul. Through lust the relative innocence of sex is abandoned. The sin of lust leads to guilt; and guilt, escaping truth, commands lust to rise. In escape from truth, sex is cultivated, not corrected. So man experiences a second fall, a third, a fourth, and so on. Through lust man's life forces dribble away.

To sin is to change, but to refuse to see what that change means in terms of sex, sickness, and dying, is to reject truth over and over again. To *stroke* sin, to comfort or sympathize with sickness, is to reinforce all the failings of pride, making all the sex-based symptoms ever more complex and dangerous. In this manner sex, as it becomes lust, breeds resentment. Resentment itself breeds lust endlessly *until death does them part.*

Out of the vicious cycle of lust and hate rise all the sicknesses and tragedies and family problems your mind can conceive. Children born of lust are beaten, despised, and rejected. Rare and beautiful are those children who are born from (relatively) innocent sex.

You can always recognize a lustful home. Cruelty, violence, and drinking are always there. Children are driven to a life of drugs and crime. Out of frustration, husbands beat their wives, wives beat on their husbands. Both abuse and degrade their children. Women degrade men through sex, and men degrade their wives through the violence to which they have been driven. Violence is a male tease, sex is a woman's.

Man inherits a powerful sexual drive through an original fall. Now, if man could honestly face up to this fact, he might not take such pride in his virility, nor would he seek worship for it. The so-called *natural, God-given* way of perpetuating himself is not too far from innocence. If a man can express his failing with a special understanding and responsibility, then that sex remains active and innocent until the coming of God's grace.

Within the framework of sex with responsibility, conscience becomes a modifying and remolding factor. Here is discipline, a sense of justice, respect for—and from—the family. Shining through innocence is the paradisiacal light, beckoning one home again.

The innocent man *never* abuses his wife. He is thoughtful and considerate of her feelings. He never promotes her for his own pleasure-taking and often denies himself for her sake. For her well-being, he lets his own selfish desire pass. Knowing that his woman's eternal life—and his own—depend on his consideration, he loves her more than he does his own feelings for her. Through unselfishly setting aside desire, *love* comes through, changing the world in which a man lives and transforming man himself.

The man of love is a man of wisdom, moderate in all his ways. The more he practices the good he knows in his heart, the more good he comes to know. His family not only experiences that goodness, it also perceives the authority behind it and responds in a special way which makes it a subject of heaven rather than of hell.

Love is the ultimate authority; where it is present, there, also, is respect. But if love is not there, there is temptation and contempt. A man becomes weak and exhausted, fighting the problems he himself spawns. The only way left for him to be strong is through animal violence. Stripped of divine, gentle authority, man compensates for his failing to be a man by evolving violent animal authority. Fear and cruelty rule the roost.

To survive, a female must become even more violent or more cunning. In her failure to cope with her husband's violence, she may become too submissive to him (which makes him worse). She also becomes bossy, violent, impatient, and irritable with her children, causing them to feel the inferiority she experiences at the hand of her husband. When the failing man does not compensate with violence, then his insolent and contemptuous family rises up and walks all over him. His choices are reduced to the twin dilemmas: dominate or be dominated, enslave or be enslaved, repress or be repressed. Without divine love, this system is the only choice you have. It is the miserable treadmill of all flesh, here today and tomorrow cast into everlasting fire. Which world evolves through and around you depends upon the inclination of your individual soul.

To become a true authority in your home, gentlemen, you must discover sex with innocence. (If you are not married, then abandon fantasy and let sex pass as best you can.) To practice sex with innocence means to bear in mind that sex is a *failing*, not a virtue. Use your wife's *services* as sparingly as possible, rather than for all they are worth. Look at your wife as a person rather than a fantasy sex object of escape and judgment. *Remember that more sex breeds less respect in your wife and less authority in your home.*

The physical evidence of sin is represented by the inherited sexual impulse. I have explained that we must view this in a special way in order to work out this problem within the holy framework of marriage. Only then can a man, through the leading of God's grace, develop progressive control over animal desires. Only through repentance will the emotions of love and hate diminish along with pride, the cause of sin.

Lust is the sexual outcrop of the *second* fall. The ancient sin of pride is amplified, as the soul regards sexual longing as a virtue to be worshiped. Escaping reality, the soul sins again and again, eluding godly sorrow and its Salvation.

Taking pride in sex sets the stage for taking pride in all other failings and sicknesses as they appear. The worst pride of all is blame. Since blame is resentment, a sin that leads to failing, this resentment inexorably brings the sinner back to lust; so when lust is loved, the woman is hated, because through her lying with him, a man's condition is made worse.

No one in his *wrong* mind believes in discipline or in self-control. Emotions must run wild to free the ego from

36

guilt, from conscience and responsibility. Therefore, lust enslaves through imagined freedoms.

Through the emotions of lust and hate, man is freed from the guilt of realizing what he is becoming *through* lust and hate. Rejecting truth through lust and hate, the prideful man can never see his own wrong. He can never see that he is out of control, because when he is teased, he imagines he is being served; he imagines he is free—but only because he has lost sight of reality. A woman teases and subdues the man through sex, and in rebellion, he subdues the female through violence. Violence is the way of Satan—to man, through woman.

If you didn't know better, you might, indeed, think that when you are served, you are in control of what is doing the serving. But what serves your lust, even if it is with fear, is in charge of what you are becoming. The hell in whores and cowards takes pride in their power to create monsters out of men. While it may seem on the surface that it is "a man's world," it really is the whore's. And while it may seem that cowards tremble before tyrants and bullies, *bullies are the cowards' special creations.* Without cowards, where would bullies be? Without whores, *beasts* could not go on thinking of themselves as men.

And there you have it laid out before you. Weakness is the spiritual basis of all wickedness—a woman having *her* way through *his* ambition and hell having its way through hers.

CHAPTER 4 They Rule Through Tease and Violence

The world could indeed be conquered by goodness and reason might prevail if we knew what goodness was. To rule, they—whoever *they* are—must, at all costs, keep us in the dark, away from such potent knowledge.

Evidence that you have not found that mysterious force of goodness lies in the way you respond to pressure and authority. The more you tremble with fear or resentment, the further you are from the source of good, and the more subject you are to the subtle intimidations and manipulations of the wicked.

Fear and resentment are the measure of your falling away from reality—reality, the original power of good over evil. Evil will always be your master, as long as you respond to it with animal emotion, the very emotion that has evolved from the mysterious fall from the power of good.

Any unreasonable response to an unreasonable pressure produces an unreasonable life, revolving around unreasonable people. Man is no longer able to respond to what is reasonable. He needs trauma to grow. He responds and surrenders to wicked pressure, because it helps evolve his pride.

To rule, you must deceive and upset, you must cause doubt and make people betray their own common sense. You must uplift and cater to egos in such a way that it causes people to follow what *appears* to be their own best interest—a glorious, selfish one, of course.

What happens when we find ourselves trapped outside the protection of good is about to unfold before your eyes. The process begins with men and women. It first happened a long time ago with Adam and Eve, but the evidence that it happened then and was passed down to us is here with us today, if you care to *part the veil of mystery*.

Haven't you noticed that you feel most alive when you are teased, excited, frightened, or degraded? And haven't you noticed how men are attracted to seductive, dominating women, how they submit to them for the reward of approval? Men seem to love unreasonable women, with their unreasonable affections and unreasonable demands.

Ask yourself now—do you enjoy being teased? Do you go so far as to tease yourself with fantasies of love and hate if there is no one handy to do it for you?

Indeed, a man enjoys being teased so much that he will tempt fate for it, pinching his wife's buttocks to get her to tease him, or say some dumb thing to provoke a bully. Where true love is not present, there *tease* is lord.

If a woman should tempt a man with the tease of sex or the tease of cruelty, and if that man *doesn't* respond with the failing of lust or the failing of anger, then she will feel safe and fulfilled with him. If, on the other hand, he encourages and takes advantage of that tease and falls down to embrace every opportunity to puff up and gratify his ego with illusions of love and the pride of judgment, then he will become a slave of the love-and-hate intrigue system where tease is lord.

Because it is conceived in temptation, the fallen nature of man requires irritation to sustain it. An effective tease destroys man's original identity, establishing a creature nature centered around its teaser-creator.

While tease actually creates failing, the process is felt, strangely, as *evolution* in the mind of the victim. And so, as the soul fails through the pride of ambition, a mortal beast rises and evolves out of what was once immortal man, generating itself through the lust for the female. Instead, man ought to be *regenerating* himself through the love of his Creator.

Tease fixates the attention, drawing the ambitious consciousness away from the truth of its failing and dying and into the deception-based flesh existence of evolving into a creature of pride.

Through excitement, tease traps the soul and sustains it within a devolving body, in a separate existence apart from God as *God* itself. A man trapped in a decaying body is grounded in the woman he used and continues to use. He is unable to love and fulfill her as he should.

Responding to the appeal of the tease, the soul becomes ensnared in a creature prison with two creaturelike sensitivities—the emotions of lust and hate. When either of these failings is accepted and excited and felt as a virtue, the pride is sustained in its descent into decadence. Accepting a failing as a virtue is itself an acceptance of a lie. This lie will, as a consequence, amplify the animal proclivity for lust and hate, one emotion leading into the other.

The mental condition that accomplishes this alteration of identity is called *psychosis*. Psychosis is a dreamy state of mind where the ego lives *securely* with its failing. In this state it can exist, hiding like a common criminal from the light it left behind, trying to escape and to avoid detection and destruction of its life of pride.

It is, therefore, necessary for any prideful (weak or violent) man to employ both teases of *sex and violence* to sustain himself in his altered state, to add change to change, while unwittingly adding escape to escape and guilt to guilt. Because of guilt, he is forever drawn away from the light toward what appears to be self-creation but is, in reality, self-destruction.

No one can recognize this process of self-destruction until he is willing to give up the selfhood of pride. Until that time, evil is seen as the servant of good, with the man drawing out the worst in a woman. Having lost the authority of grace, man finds himself trapped with a woman-boss, her power sustained through the tease of sex and the tease of cruelty.

Because of an obvious physical disadvantage, a woman's ego survival has come down to depend upon guile to get her way or to maintain a semblance of security with a man. She holds a man through the sexual tease and its consequent failing, resentment, which aggravates a sexual failing that can now be more easily aroused and teased.

Where man once had authority through grace and love, he now must resort to animal violence to reassert his authority over woman. Here is where the woman can become converted into a submissive psychotic (like a man), addicted to the tease of cruelty and violence for *her* false sense of well-being and sense of becoming. The more she responds to his temptation, the more her fear (lack of faith) feeds the violent and lustful power of the *beast*.

When a man gives in to her tease, it makes a woman feel cheated, frustrated, and angry. So it is with a woman giving in to the violence of a man. *Giving in* is never love. It is weakness! It is a subtle form of use!

Rebelling against her psychotic state, the woman can reassert her authority violently with the beast evolved from her husband. And so, between the psychosis of sex and the psychosis of violence, a world of hell evolves into the home and husband and wife destroy one another.

The more ambitious a man is, the more he needs a woman in order to achieve; he needs her to console him in the failing of achievement and the failing of failing. Men *on top* are ruthless, as are their women; and men and women *on the top* rule their culture through the politics of sex and violence, utilizing what they cultivate from one another.

Families are either dictatorships or democracies. Democracies live under the rule of seduction, of sexual politics. On the surface, things seem to go well, but the exploitation of sexual politics sets the stage for violent revolution followed by dictatorships, where tyrants rule and exploit with the politics of violence. Germany under Hitler was an example of this kind of love-hate intrigue, which spilled over and out of the *family* and almost destroyed the world.

As long as you have any pride left, you continue existing under the spell of Original Sin, loving lust and lusting for hate, dying under the system God prepared for those who reject him. The psychotic has no choice but to model himself after the unreasonable source of his re-creation.

Psychotic people stimulate themselves with the fantasies of love or the fantasies of violence (judgment). The lower they sink, the more tease preys on their minds. If psychotics let go of the stimulation inherent in imagination (originally inspired by corrupt associations), their bubble would burst and lay bare their sick souls rooted and wallowing in folly and horror.

Psychotics fear waking up, because their loving souls are afraid of truth and afraid to *die*. Remember, real death appears as life to the ego, while true life appears as dying. The light of reality slays pride in its realm of illusion, while emotion-based deception sustains the ego in its animal existence with delusions of grandeur.

Seeking out sex or violence is a soul-consuming way of *life* for man, a total preoccupation with death and dying as though it were life and living.

Tease is like soul food, something that satisfies the lust of the soul for the judgment which rises from feelings of love and hate. Resentment is a tasty morsel for the psychotic soul. Sin becomes an experience, a memory one can relive again and again. While the psychotic "cow" chews the cud of memory, the teaser sucks away the milk of life.

There are those professional liars and teasers who make a living out of dying. There are those who are perpetual victims, laboring under the illusion that they are served and catered to like kings, while they are milked like cows.

Let me show you the details of how violence, in its turn, produces the hypnotic emotion of resentment, how it indoctrinates and poisons the soul, debasing succeeding generations into creature slaves subject to hell's authority. Here then is the psychology of violence as a means of making and keeping men slaves.

[Edited transcript of one of Roy Masters' radio tirades on the subject of the hypnosis of violence]:

I often become tongue-tied when I am obliged to talk on mundane matters. But when it comes to spiritual things, then my mind becomes alive and awake.

Last evening I turned the TV channels, scanning for meaningful tidbits and pieces of information, as is my custom. It is surprising how much you can glean from the media if you know how. Television brings the *crazy world* into your living room without your having to suffer it in the flesh. As I watch this garbage, I often find I am unable to keep my mind on what is going on or what they're saying.

Driving along, sometimes I listen to those silly talk show hosts, to people calling in to discuss this subject or that And—my God!—I find I can't track with it. It is astounding how they can keep up such an endless barrage of verbal garbage. But every now and then, a little meaty flicker jumps out at me, and that sets me thinking about what they are up to.

Last evening I watched the educational channel concerning the story of the voyages of Charles Darwin. Darwin encountered some slavery in his travels in Brazil. There was a scene depicting a "Christian" overlord, the owner of a plantation, allowing his foreman to be cruel with a little black child. Poor Darwin was shown to be very appalled.

As I watched this dramatization of universal cruelty toward an innocent child, I saw more clearly the reason behind all cruelty, and I turned off the TV to contemplate what had been revealed. Here is the principle in a nutshell:

The entire purpose behind cruelty is to enslave. Cruelty throws a person into a psychotic state *through the victim's own resentment*, representing as it does an inherent weakness of the soul. The inability to cope with the horror of stress expresses a lack of grace, or faith. Without the response of grace (which is the response of no response at all), one is left with the response of pride that enslaves one to tease.

Slaves are created and imprisoned by the inherent weakness of their own pride. Resentment sustains pride in its animal form, as tease sustains resentment. The slave surrenders in order to spoil his master into being a greater object of hate on which the slave can model himself.

To expand the concept of enslavement through cruelty, let me say that cruelty hypnotically excites the psychotic state of fear and resentment, where the ego of the little sinner feels served by the greater weakness of the bigger sinner. Pride must be served tease in order to grow.

Just look around and see how much cruelty there is in factories, homes, and schools, and observe the various psychotic states and emotional problems of young and old. All this is a direct result of the overlord parent, teacher, or feudal boss playing God, projecting a psychotic state in order to establish and maintain power over the victim.

The second villain in the Darwin story was the foreman of the ranch, a cruel but otherwise *people-pleasing* peasant, himself a slave of a cruel master. As his master was with him, he was with the boy—weak before the strong, strong before the weak. He couldn't bow low enough to this master, but in the presence of the child, he took on his master's personality. Before the child his pleasant, appeasing attitude and demeanor changed and became ugly.

Life is a wretched dog-eat-dog chain gang of victims. We are all weak before the strong and strong before the weak. Because we are weak before the strong, we acquire, through failing, the character of those who corrupt us. The worst kind of taskmaster is one who is himself a slave. Through failing we learn about our weakness, but instead of conquering it, we turn around and do unto others as was done unto us. We learn to lord it over other people by using their weakness against them.

We do not develop much understanding about our slave role, because the psychotic state forbids our seeing failing as failing. With carnal knowledge evolved from our encounter with hell, we perpetuate power through suffering and cruelty. In this fashion the system of man's enslavement of man through man's inhumanity to man is perpetuated down through the centuries. We seem to acquire the mysteries of hell's power by falling to it and rising again as lords over others.

Few people know much about the nature of their own enslavement, because they are so distracted—so busy becoming like what they enjoy hating. The psychotic bent for the forbidden prevents the truth from entering in and awakening the soul.

The sheer agony, the horror, of what we have become through responding to cruelty and becoming cruel makes the light of reality seem more cruel than cruelty itself. Shame and guile then compel us to stay emotionally asleep in our psychotic dream state—reality being more terrifying to the guilty than hell. Under cover of the night of unawareness, the unholy spirit takes up residence in us and we become unto others as others were unto us.

See how easy it is for me to speak in spiritual terms? How very hard it is for me to remember nonsense! I find it almost impossible to concentrate on the proliferation of garbage that is in the world and all its meaningless chatter. I am often accused of being absentminded, because it all goes right by me. There is no room for any of it to bleed into my head. But your problem is just the opposite.

All that garbage *does* leak into your mind, displacing understanding. Resentment—the response to violence—pushes understanding out. You become more and more sensitive to everything, and it fills your mind like water filling a sinking ship. The sanctity of your soul is torn open!

You are meant to go through life like a boat gliding through water. The boat goes through the water; the water does not go through the boat! You must go through experience; experience must not go through you.

You must not collect your nature from experience with tease and temptation, or else you will be filled with its nature. People must be awakened from the psychotic state in which the various forms of temptation have placed them.

America is the last great bastion of freedom, the most important republic. But I look around me and I see how low it has fallen. What an absurd thing they have made of freedom! People walking around in various psychotic states, each imagining—in his drugged state of booze, sex, music, whatever—that he is free. In such a psychotic state of slavery, we can be made to believe that we are free, but we are free only from the truth that we are slaves in the psychotic state of hell.

We enslave one another with subtle cruelties and drive one another to seek answers in religion, pot, music, politics, medicine. Each of us lives within a miniature feudal system as either a king or a slave, provoking tease and being provoked by tease. We do not know how to deal with the system under which we suffer—the job, the federal government, the oil company, whatever—each projecting its own form of cruelty and frustration and inducing its own psychotic addiction.

Upset at work, we each go home as the *lord* of our own system (if we are lucky). We lay down our own unreasonable rules, and we do our own exploiting and aggravating through them.

There is only one hope, one way we can be free from the tyrannies which are engulfing us all, and that is to find a way to change our *human* nature. We must truly learn the meaning of suffering. We must awaken from our suffering to deal with the *source* of that suffering—the emotional obligation to respond to the pressure and persuasion of our peers.

If you fail to cope with the evil of authority, if you believe and respond to it, then you must be content to remain asleep in guilt. Through the door of pleasure come genocide and the gas ovens of dictatorship. Democracies, like pleasure-centered marriages, must descend to become dictatorships; it is inevitable.

We are not ourselves. We are projections of someone else's psychosis. Every *dog* becomes a *god* to others down the line. With others we can remember that we are lords and forget we are slaves. We pass this evil on down the chain and through succeeding generations until a few of us awaken to what we are doing.

There is no length or breadth or depth to which we will not sink for the pleasure of harming and the enjoyment of being harmed. Think of it! We can actually enjoy being corrupted, because we feel that we are becoming and acquiring the secrets of power. Trauma is growing and evolving for the pride; we need trauma to grow and to forget what grew. *To forget what grew is to grow even more.*

One of the founding fathers said that democracy gives every man the right to be his own dictator. Democracies degenerate, forming a pyramid out of the stinking, helpless masses, with the most bizarre sexual or violent symbol or motivator at the top.

We are *all* immensely cruel toward one another. There isn't one single person reading this who isn't a victim of a victim of a victim, passing power back up the chain of command to the original hellion who passes down his nature and authority in the commerce of sin.

The horrors are steadily mounting up to the sky. The pain of suffering is so great for those on the bottom of the pyramid that it often forces them to dramatize their dreams of judgment through mindless violence.

Prison is a microcosm of society. The thoughtlessness of prison guards and warden bureaucracy is the subtle cruelty from which evolves rage, and from which there is no relief save violence. If you have ever been in a prison, you know what it's like. Guards are worse than the criminals, and the warden himself is usually the chief instigator of revolt against him. In his own special way, by laying down cruel and thoughtless rules, phony and meaningless regulations, the warden represents the cruel bureaucracy of the outside world that drove the inmates to crime in the first place. He could, of course, have decent, commonsense rules, but they don't tempt. And without temptation there is no satisfaction of power.

The IRS could have commonsense rules to make life easier for people. Instead, they make it all the more complicated. Why do those in power make it complicated? Because they accumulate more power by creating guilt and frustration, driving the population into psychotic states of submission, like the little slave boy in the story. People submit for relief until there is nothing more to give, and then they commit suicide or rebel, with an even more wicked head at the helm after whom they model themselves.

The power trip wears many guises: politics, medicine, religion; you name it. You know—those who pretend to help you but help themselves *to* you instead. There is the petty tyrant who enjoys needling you and walking away high, feeling better.

The typical bureaucrat is a psychotic failure who bows down to his master, conforming so completely as to be *knighted* by his master's blessing of power. With unreasonable rules and regulations, such people make our lives bitter. They may not get rich, but they enjoy the feeling of importance that enforcing unreasonable regulations brings to them.

There is a secret, bizarre pleasure in making complicated and stupid rules and regulations, in making miles of red tape to tangle people in and make their lives miserable, in creating problems that need more bureaucratic problem-solvers.

There is a secret high in driving people into psychotic states. Eventually, though, there comes the inevitable backlash of sickness, depression, suicide, and revolution.

Modern life has become increasingly complicated; emotional problems are on the rise. The prisons and mental hospitals are overflowing. In their frustration with government, parents take their hostilities out on their children. Blacks kill blacks, husbands and wives murder each other at an alarming rate. Children are driven to drugs and beating old ladies for kicks. Why? Because of the subtle *snake* in power, who (in a democracy) may not be overtly cruel but is cruel by virtue of stupid rules and regulations *designed to intimidate and irritate and frustrate, to drive the population into psychotic states of submission.* Power is the name of the game.

The face of evil doesn't always wear a Hitler-type mask. It keeps changing, so that as soon as you learn to cope with one form it appears in another. It may be concealed behind smiling bureaucrats or seductive, lying hypocrites, giving the kind of religious or medical advice that never leads anywhere except to more frustration, anger, resentment, futility, and despair, all of which make everyone need more law, more regulation, and more religion.

Beware! You are all up against some very subtle and dangerous forces. The real villains are hard to catch! The real villains behind the riots at these state prisons and the real instigators of revolution are not the revolutionaries themselves. The real devils have merely set the stage;

52

they are the ones who appear as *pillars of society*, doing their best, doing their job, sitting behind desks, making those stupid, frustrating rules and regulations to which we all respond angrily, as we psychotically conform and rebel against conformity. The real villain is a spirit of evil that lives in the ambitions of men and women.

That's why it is important for all of us to understand why you must be *aware* of your own debilitating, enslaving emotional response. The *love* you need works against you, and so does the resentment you need.

Evil aspires to power through government and the underworld—two horns on the same devil, one form evolving the other. A government of sinners is an underworld, and an underworld is a government of sinners; one gives rise to the other, and they sustain one another. Somewhere in between are the great masses of society, conforming and rebelling, lending their strength to the evolving extremes of power. That is why things are so hopeless for you.

[end transcript]

Man no longer answers to reason, but responds pridefully to unreasonable pressure, endowing it with a peculiar power to become more unreasonably wicked, to sustain him in his appetite for tease. You will surrender to all the wrong people; you will spoil them rotten to get them to tease you.

Look what happens when you are tempted to do something you shouldn't. You get caught—fall into the hands of the law. It is a terrible thing to fall prey to the machinery of crime and then fall into the machinery of punishment. You become further victimized by the machinery of lawyers, those parasites of the human race who help you to become caught up in the heartless machinery of institutions and "corrections," where you continue to fail and fall into the hands of wicked judges who revel in the judgment seat and drive you deeper into frustration and into criminal psychosis. *It is a terrible thing to be delivered into the hand of man!* Surely you will come out of their institutions a lot worse than you went in—more insane, a sick revolutionary, a criminal, perhaps.

If you knew what grace was in the first place, you would not have been trapped in the second place. It is your emotion-based suggestibility that delivers you into this hell of man's help. Find your way back to grace, and you will come out from under the destructive system of responding to tease and the necessary evils of regulations and controls.

Human failing has made regulation necessary and increasingly complex, because the more wrong you become, the more you need religion, medicine, and law. Regulations eventually become so insane that you could conceivably get on a bus one day and unknowingly break some law. Eventually the law itself encroaches upon human rights and takes away the freedoms it is supposed to protect. When that happens, the law shows its true colors.

As you know, people can be controlled through guilt. To make everyone guilty, all that must be done is to make the laws so completely unreasonable that everyone becomes a criminal. Do you see how government, politicians, and lawyers can confuse you? Are you already out of control by being controlled? If so then *1984* is near!

Sin makes law a necessary evil. While we can't live without the law, neither can we always live with it; we need grace. The necessary evil of the law is showing its face now, with innocent people going to jail and guilty ones going free. Eventually the masses see the law for the subtle trap that it really is. Then many terrible things happen; law and order break down, people side with violent social saviors, and criminal dictators take over. Perhaps the law and the lawless join forces and society collapses, but one way or another the grand design of the devil appears on earth as it is in hell.

What can we do about the lesser evil of law and the greater evil of lawlessness and all those *mad social scientists*? Doesn't bigger government make for greater crime—requiring more government? Pity the poor people who are caught in between. The mental hospitals and jails are overflowing.

Do you see why you must not fall into the machinery of these miniature hells? Do you see why you must be so poised, so above it all, that you do not ever rise and then fall to challenge, to sexual tease, to resentment and judgment? You must be complete and, thus, poised beyond the reach of temptation in your mind. You must become inwardly immune to the *mad hatters* of culture whose cure for one problem is the cause of a dozen others. Without grace you wander aimlessly from one extreme emotion to the other, with no real future, no escape, giving government power to run you and ruin you, giving power to social and criminal psychopaths.

You must speak to your children about this. Tell them that morality, patience, and self-control are not toys, not inventions of imagination, but *living principles* given to protect us all from the Evil One. They are meant to keep us safe and sound from the twin evils of justice and crime, as well as the madnesses of medicine, religion, and false friends.

Teach your children to be thoughtful, honest, and patient and not to play around or experiment with the drugs of dope, sex, and music. You should love and protect your children from undue excitement and cruelty, especially your own. Never take your frustrations out on them. You must stress that morality leads to salvation from the evils of crime and punishment. Only through morality can the nightmare of this world come to an end.

Law rises to govern the lawless, and that law has no heart. If any noble soul rises to power, it will be only by some magic of God's grace—pray that one does!

You all form the base of the pyramid of oppression. Authority feeds on your failing to deal with it, your crazy lust, your blind anger and judgments. You fall further and further from grace to need all the laws of man. The kind of people who build cages for your children have a different face from those who encourage them to break the law. Banks need bank robbers. Disease calls forth medicine. Rulers and criminal psychopaths belong to the same world and could not exist without one another. Through sickness and crime, men of letters enlarge their kingdom, each in his own beguiling way, ruling through the frustrating rules and answers that their respective offices produce.

Warn the young people!! Help them understand that WE, the people lost in sin, lost in fantasy, without faith, are the cause of our own oppression—for as surely as we fail, we draw those who lord it over us up from hell to make our lives a misery.

Without faith in what we *know* is right in our hearts, we have no ground to resist the wicked. We respond resentfully to all their subtle injustice. We become confused, crazy, sick, violent, and then they have us in their grasp. Look, then, to what we say to ourselves: *I must be angry, or else they will walk all over me.* But when you are upset, you have only the energy of a mad dog. A beast evolves, not a person. Then comes guilt that makes you afraid to be angry, and that in turn causes pressure to build up inside; so you give in anyway. But when you give in, *that* is what they are waiting for—for you to give yourself over to them. That only makes you angry all over again, rebelling and conforming, conforming and rebelling, endlessly, hopelessly, despairingly.

Into this system, Jesus Christ came to save you. He himself was not under that order of things. He was not subject to crime or punishment. Through his faith in what he knew was right in his heart, he broke the back of the powers of the law. *Remember, Jesus Christ was an innocent man, persecuted for his integrity, and his reward for helping people become free of the law was death; he was murdered "legally."* He came to bring the world back to the Creator, to save the world from sin and the need for the law. The law killed him for that. The spirit of the law in those days was the same as the spirit of the law is now.

That same seductive spirit is presently eating the heart out of nations, heaping terrible burdens and rebellions on the people. Through taxes and other subtle social cruelties, it causes terrible frustrations and makes people turn on one another. It creates its own criminal element that justifies its existence. The law cannot save, it can only restrain and robotize.

Through its condemnation of Christ, the law itself came under judgment. The legal system of the world is now under judgment. Under grace you are above the law, exposing the law to its shame and making it harmless. Find grace and discover the meaning, and you shall know (experience) the truth and the Truth shall make you free from the teases of love and hate and crime and punishment.

CHAPTER 5 The Torture of Selfish Commitment

I have a problem in a relationship with a girl I have been going out with. I have been listening to your program, and I have your books and tapes. I can see some past performances in my life. I am reflecting on one of these—an especially highly intensive, psychotic episode. I was very intensely involved with my work. Anyway, I got divorced. I quit my job and took time to reestablish myself.

Roy Masters: Are you telling me that it is your habit to become involved in everything you do?

Yes—totally. I don't want to do that anymore.

Have you any idea what you are doing—getting lost like that? You are escaping from yourself to find yourself. You are escaping from yourself one way to find yourself in another. You escape the reality of your failing in order to find yourself in a more ego-satisfying, complementary way.

I can fully identify with that.

This is the classic folly of pride, endlessly repeating itself in every lifestyle, becoming more deeply involved and identified with people, places, and things, until it dies. All escape experiences are traumas. Every

59

trauma produces an apparent benefit that is later seen for what it is. Employing the excitement of trauma, the soul sins; reemploying another trauma, the soul forgets that it has sinned. Growing like an animal, caught up in the process of forgetting, the soul cannot realize that it is creating more of the problem of guilt to escape from again.

Yes. I can fully identify with what you are saying. There is one situation I have been working on, trying to improve what I am doing and watching myself more closely; I am at the point of reentering into business life, due to new business opportunities. This time I want to do it right, but I fear I have not been very good at maintaining relationships with women.

What man is?

That gives me comfort.

I didn't mean to give you comfort!

I have been going out with a girl, and I am beginning to see that the key to the happiness I seek deals with commitment.

It does, indeed. But commitment must always begin with a deep sense of responsibility to what is right in your heart first; only then can you be committed to others without being their slave.

Drug addicts are committed to drugs as religious fanatics are committed to their gurus. During the war, Japanese soldiers who were committed to their emperor-god killed themselves for his approval. So be very careful in what you mean by commitment. Commitment is not necessarily a thing of honor. It is, more often than not, a very self-serving, selfish thing.

We are coming closer to what I want to know. I am totally aware of what you are saying. I don't want to get so involved with anyone or anything that it will absorb me.

60

Who does? But that is bound to happen when you are selfish and prideful. You become absorbed, identified, imprinted, enslaved to sex, drugs, work—anything. Self-serving, ego-gratifying commitments involve use, not love, and so they are always dangerous forms of escape from guilt into the ego-reinforcing process.

Escape from guilt is a guilt to escape from; that is why you become a slave. You can become so thoroughly changed and so guilty, that you will be afraid to wake up to realize the truth of what you are becoming.

I pulled back and I saw this in my relationship with her; so I told her *Well, let me go out with other women, and you go out with other men.* I have been telling her this for a month, but basically, I really haven't gone out anywhere myself.

Now we are getting around to the problem.

Yes; last night she had a date.

Are you married to her?

No.

Well, then, what is the problem? You're jealous! And you're angry.

That's it!

Have you had a sexual relationship with her?

Yes.

I thought so. Well, then, he has just been into what you've been into—if you will pardon the expression. He has defiled your personal god, your ground of being, your personal source of existence. Every ego that loses itself to "find" itself again, whether it be a guru or a girlfriend, makes that personality object its idol or model. This man has defiled your idol with his filth. What happens to her happens to you. If she

61

debases herself with him, then it threatens you in spirit. She is your personal god, one that you have anointed to acknowledge and worship you. You are identified with her and with what happens to her.

I am having difficulty in being able to cope with that fact, relating it to this *god game* concept.

Every ego aspiring to the godhead desires to see itself in a special light as that something special; but there is another true light which every ego fears, the light of truth. So there are two forces courting the soul, and two realms. Depending upon the inclination of your soul, you identify with one or the other.

You can wake up from the dream of pride and see yourself as you are, in the true light. Here, in your ego, you can no longer go on being proud. You can repent of pride and change. In this case, your pridefulness withers away before its time, and the creature self also crumbles and falls apart to nothing.

The prideful ego that fears being nothing cannot survive in this inner light. It has to run for cover, into distraction, company, and the security of the flesh. In your pridefulness and stubbornness you have no other choice but to involve yourself in another presence. You are compelled to escape from the unbearable pain of reality of a greater light, so that ego-creature self might experience a sense of survival in its dying.

To preserve the image creature, you must lose yourself in a tease—a person, a place, or a thing. If you enjoy building beautiful boats, the involvement with your work becomes an escape. Eventually the finished product evolves to testify to the greatness of it maker. Like a god with his creation, you are identified with this boat.

What happens to the boat happens to you! And you can become depressed if the boat sinks. Losing yourself in sex will produce the same effect when you lose your woman.

In order to obtain this effect, evolving and becoming a beautiful, proud beast, you must first debase yourself by involving yourself through experience. Remember, that is also how you become addicted.

The experience that makes you grow pridefully (and which later makes you forget what grew) binds you to it. Any person, place, or thing which makes you feel that you are something which you are not substitutes for God, the god you yourself want to become by creating and identifying with it. You must give that god the power to excite your involvement; otherwise, you cannot escape or identify with the beautiful work or grow as a beautiful god yourself. Everything you use for escape you are bound to give power to tease or torment you, to change you and your image.

The point is that whatever or whoever plays this game is not really a serving god but an enslaving god. It will at first seem to be a lesser god created to recognize you as the greater one. If your habit is to escape into work, then you will become absorbed in your work, your boat, whatever. You will become your boat, and you will feel guilty, lost, and afraid without it. You misinterpret your guilt to mean unfaithfulness to your work, when it is, in fact, unfaithfulness to God.

From the egocentric point of view, everything that caters to your ego, everything which allows you to lose yourself in it, everything which fulfills your need to feel important and which seems to serve captures the soul. What you use for this purpose uses you, consumes you. What seemed to be the servant and the subject becomes your master.

Maybe I've been trying to fight in the direction you're going. In being so close, I've tried to pull back. I suppose that is why I encouraged her to go out—until it came time for her to go.

Of course. You are lying to yourself. How can you give up what your ego needs to grow? You must go on using it to avoid seeing that you are enslaved to it.

I remember I once knew an overprotective mother. Her son of twenty-five or twenty-six years hadn't left home yet. She had weakened him by her phony love. She had set him up, re-created a man in her image. She loved playing God to her son, she needed him for that purpose; and of course, he was so hopelessly corrupted by his mother that he had a similar relationship with her that a male has with a female. She had the upper hand.

Anytime he sensed his mother's wicked selfishness and suspected she had some kind of hold on him, she would counter that by appearing generous: Now, son, I want you to go out and find a nice girl and get married and not stay with your mother all the time. *It sounded like she really wanted him to leave home. All it did was make him feel like a heel. It made him doubt himself and made him fall from his own confidence to depend on her approval.*

Men depend on their mothers' approval when they are growing up, but when they realize how they are enslaved, they escape to a wife who starts out by serving them and ends up by enslaving too.

Many games are played by wives and mothers to hold on to their prey. This young man was "married" to his mother. Her ploy worked every time. He didn't know how to deal with her deceit. When he detected it, he resented it. The resentment became a new tease. When he felt guilty before his god, he would involve himself with her for approval. He needed her more and more because of the resentment addiction.

But the longer he lingered, the more she put her nature inside him and the more he needed her in order to be a complete person. He was, of course, becoming a complete woman rather than a complete man. But he was afraid of being without her, because she was all he was and had to be. Whatever he was, that had to be the truth. That same principle applies in any use relationship.

I think she really wanted to stay, and I said no.

Perhaps she did, but you didn't really mean what you said. It was a game. Perhaps you wanted to free yourself from enslavement by getting her to commit a wrong first, to relieve you of a bond of obligation. But then when she did, you felt the pain of her experience and your freedom. You felt resentment, and this sin of guilt amplified the sin of need for her.

Would it have been better if I had been honest?

It is always good to be straight, but I don't want to get into that now. That is a psychology in itself.

What consoles, comforts, and caters to your pride displaces the real you with another you that cries out for what spawned it. Through various friendships you slowly become it, and it becomes you. Because it dominates, you can't live with it, but neither can you exist without it.

Your worship is a need for wickedness. It is a roundabout way of worshiping and becoming yourself, bringing a prideful being into existence, but it backfires!

65

Only the wrong in a lover will rise to serve the wrong in you, and the wrong in them becomes you. This relationship turns out to be not a thing of beauty after all, but an ugliness from which you must escape.

Alas, you are bound to worship in order to escape and to exist. You can only exist with and as that thing—the wrong—the thing from which you experience need and hate. To preserve yourself, your pride must escape from you. Instead of getting better, you become worse. It is a vicious cycle.

It is an unworthy self that seeks to preserve or acquire a sense of worth with all the wrong people. *You can never, ever be at peace. You begin to fear being alone; having nothing to cling to is like not existing. Alone with your true self, you must see that you are not what you think you are; you are a shadowy, evil thing. Alone, without the tease of love and the tease of cruelty, you fall apart.*

As long as you are emotional and selfish, you cannot experience anything without evolving the sick nature of pride. Until the soul is committed to seek the purpose for which it was created and abandons the struggle to know itself as God, then it is bound to one trauma-serving devil after another, devils that awaken the soul to the sensuous dream of pride. You must be involved; you must escape for the relief of guilt and to trigger the evolution of the ego creature apart from God as god itself. If you are not committed right, then you've committed wrong. If you don't have a true soul mate, you are stuck with a cell mate.

Then, where can you find a balanced relationship?

Where there is a selfish need, there is only unbecoming use. There can be no balance, because true balance is lost when you selfishly "fall in love"; you really fall from what that love is all about.

66

You never become what you think. You become a dog instead of a god. There is this dog, this creature self you don't want to face. The light of reality is ever present to show you what a dog you are. But escape, you must, and so you slip into something more comfortable. *This* something *reinforces the dog self in you as if it were the god self—ape as though it were a man.*

Now you see it, now you don't. It is a magical vicious cycle to which all self-seeking souls are chained. It is a nature all beguilers can manipulate. They understand the weakness for evil of both men and women. They understand the original love affair with lies. Man's prideful craving for the female ground of being need only be exploited and expanded to achieve total control over mankind.

Madison Avenue understands the female-based, evil-centered God game. They know that the secret way to a man's mind is through a woman's body. The Serpent in the Garden is the present-day snake in the grass. The sensual body is the manifestation of the failing of the soul. The body evolves and rises each time the soul fails. Since the soul's failing has separated it from its true ground of being, it becomes subject to the forces and feelings growing up in the body. As the body becomes subject to the conditions of the world, so is the soul manacled to a woman's tease.

Then where do you find the balance?

Your need for others represents a selfishness, a prideful selfish use of a person to fulfill an unconscious ancient purpose. When you are involved in people, places, and things for illusions of pride, there can only be unbalance and the evolution of death through tragedy.

Pride is dependent on the devil for its security. When you are motivated by pride, you cease to exist as a child of the light. You become earthy and sensual—old, diseased, and ugly. You are feverishly committed to forever running from the truth of what you have become, selfishly abusing yourself with everything you can, giving yourself over more and more completely to exchange the lie of truth for the truth of lies and the false life that rises from lies.

Your only choice is between the flesh pot of escape and the cold light of reality. You reach away from one to find the other. You make love to life and life makes love to you. Tempting people to tempt you is the experience you crave, a little bit of death coming "alive."

Every commitment you make to your food, your women, your wine, your country—everything that is not based upon a commitment to your Creator first—is a selfish commitment in the secret service of selfishness, and only the devil will play along. He will give you gold stars and Brownie buttons for dumb loyalties.

Men think of this enslavement, this need to be fulfilled by momma, religion, country, whore, as true devotion. But when they are fulfilled by momma, there is more of momma in them. Their sick, beguiling spirit calls outside to momma for more life that is more death. Soon the beast in them is even less willing to face up to reality. The soul must spend more time dreaming up a helpmate in its creature mind, burying itself deeper in the evolving flesh in serving momma—momma drink, momma drug, momma music, momma country.

You are always escaping and identifying. When one addiction is discovered for what it is (a form of slavery, destructive rather than helpful, enslaving rather than serving), then you may look for something else to escape into. Whatever provides this service becomes the next enslavement and injects a little more poison into your soul. Slowly everything takes a little piece of the real you away. In its place a sick, evil, poison-loving old creature rises up from the earth, ready for death and the grave. At that time you may see whom you have been doing business with all along. You might have resisted, had you known the truth, but when death calls, it is an ultimate temptation you cannot resist. It is too late.

When a man is committed in his heart to serve the purpose for which he was created, he begins to see his own selfishness. He sees how this selfish ego need can only develop if he corrupts himself with sin through the twin traumas of love and hate. As pride and selfishness develop, there evolves a need that can never be satisfied.

Wife abuse, religion abuse, drug abuse—all are secret self-abuses. We abuse to be abused. We do this for the sake of coming "alive," for a sense of belonging and of identity. In a flash the seeking soul sees all those commitments not as love or goodness, but as a little baby evil crying out for reassurance of a greater evil. "Recognize me," it cries, "and I will be good (God) to you. Tell me how great I am! I will take pride in serving you and cause earthy flesh to spread over your bones to become God incarnate." We seek intrigues of sex and violence. We ask, we beg, for trouble through our fighting and "loving."

The ego has a love affair with deceit. Hitler used deceit to gain power. He created both followers and victims with his lies. Every politician who has opened his wicked mouth uses the same principle of intrigue, promising what he cannot deliver. Victims love being victims, and followers love to be followers. They "dig" loving and love hating, and truth threatens the whole bloody lot. Tell a person how great he is, and he will follow you to the end of the earth. Then reveal the face of cruelty, and watch his ego enjoy hating it.

Through being a love-hate object of trauma, the devil gets the power he wants, and the people get the illusion of life they want. Turn on the television any day and there you will find deceivers telling people how great they are and how much God loves them. What kind of god is this that comforts us? What manner of god is it that excites emotions and reinforces the wrong in us as if it were right? What god is this that keeps us from true repentance and true Salvation? Surely it is the god of the underworld that shields us from the light?

Where is this light?

The Light is ever present within you, showing you the reason you suffer. It is because of sin—the sin of pride—pride aspiring and failing, pride that sees backward, perceiving all failing as rising. As you come to face reality, you see that your "love" attraction to the world has made you God's mortal enemy. You will realize that you are not missing anything by giving up that fatal affection. You are not being cold or disloyal in abandoning those sensual obligations, affections, and love affairs.

Once the false love bug bites, something in you is lost that you didn't know you had before you were bitten! Now you miss your lover, who is really your corrupter. You must degrade yourself before a lover and try to absorb her more deeply to find your missing part. Then when you find that you have been absorbed and betrayed

70

instead, you start hating. There goes a little bit more of your real self, in comes some more of your rotten self. You try to pull yourself away from your beloved, but you can't, because you have come down into a system of life and pride that demands her presence. In your futile striving for glory, you are like a Las Vegas loser, hoping but losing in that hope, that being all the hope you have.

Now let me tell you what to do. I have some records to teach you to meditate. Use them. All you need to do is to learn this one simple thing.

What I have been talking about is a psychology of failure rooted around one general principle of pride, reinforcing itself in you either through ignorance of your origin or just plain stupidity and arrogance. In your failing state your ego mistakes the source to which you must devote yourself. You reinforce a failing self as though it were gloriously rising to completion.

Are you now referring to sex?

Yes. Original Sin is pride. The physical manifestation or evidence of this ego failing is the sex impulse. To feel less guilty about sex, pride gravitates to that which originally altered man's human nature with lies to accept and comfort him and, through that sexual comfort, sustain him in his prideful existence. Although sex is not necessarily a sin, if not understood it can be used as an ego boost, becoming a sin of pride. Then sex goes on changing the man into an animal, compelling him to forget what he is becoming with lust, drugs, and drink.

Alcohol gives a drunk the same kind of freedom from truth that sex can. Every drunk is a guilty swine, every drug addict is a guilty swine, and no guilty swine wants to face that truth. So he takes a nosedive into experiencing

71

some object of worship. The pleasurable nosedive produces a trauma of escape into the sin of becoming a prideful creature. He has no real love or feeling for anyone; everyone and everything is eyed as an object of use.

We are forever trying to escape the people we use. Whoever we use is able to use our use of him. Remember, I have said that the act of being degraded or degrading oneself actually feels like god creating himself and coming into existence. Any sin experience provides the catalyst for the evolution of pride and forgetfulness. We forget we are not God and remember that we are!

Once corrupted, the soul is drawn back to the original scene of the crime to find an ecstasy of escape into "self-discovery," a completion of the original prideful self implanted by the original sin experience. Prideful man needs more and more trauma and more lies to create those traumas. He is committed to falling and changing, forgetting what a pig he is, thinking what a great, wonderful creature he is becoming. He leads a sensual life based on deceit.

Surely there is a way to coexist with women properly?

Of course there is. But first of all you must know what it means to coexist with your Creator. He must save you from the woman so you can save her from herself. A woman can no more resist the temptation to support a weak man than a cardshark can resist a sucker who fancies he is lucky at cards. The presence of a weak man excites the serpent in her to play the Eve game. She is the house, and the man is the gambler, sacrificing himself for an elusive gain. Her body must serve the man if she is to *rule him. Without his true love, Eve can't help but rise to mother his weakness. She needs the sense of security and power that comes from playing that ancient role; it's all she has with him.*

He may think he is the boss—she lets him believe it but is damn sure that she is in charge! He looks at her with longing and need and she feels the hell coming up to claim them both. She is changing now. She is part he, part she, and part demon. The unholy trinity: a mockery of the Father, Son, and Holy Spirit. She is the "son" made in the image of hell, and he is formed out of the "man," the female reflection of the Satan spirit. Everything is in reverse of God's plan.

Seek, therefore, the true ground of being. To find it, you must be willing to give up pride, emotion, and fantasy. Imagination is the world where pride lives away from reality, where you are the only reality. That is a very dangerous place to be. When you are lost in your mind, words take on false life and false meaning; they lie, they excite. Here you are like God, in control of everything. It seems as though you are making people serve you. But you are merely giving power to devils to excite you with lies, with words, with the knowledge of good and evil.

What are these concepts, these ideas of development where you use your imagination creatively in business and industry?

Your imaginative mind is a computer. You are not supposed to live inside your computer; otherwise, you lose control over the input. Lost in your imagination, your computer is overshadowed by other forces suggesting exciting lies and ideas to you. You are no longer creating in a godly sense, but in a prideful and tragic sense.

Because you cannot see the truth, you will believe these ideas to be originating from you. In your supreme pride, you may even blame yourself when things go wrong, because if you believe you are God, then you must be responsible. You could even cure the problem the only way a god can—by killing yourself. Your death is Satan's purpose for living. Your dying is his existence. Do you understand more now?

Yes.

Of course you do. You see, through pride, you're a fallen being—

But you overwhelm me. You don't give me much of a chance to get back up.

I am not striking at you, but at the "not you." The real you comes forward and meditates. All I want you to do is to be still. You will find the new, antitraumatic experience that will lead you out of your imagination realm to Salvation. To bring you to the truth, we must speak about what opposes your coming to that truth. No one can come to the truth except by understanding where they fail. You live pridefully—too much in your imagination, which is the refuge for your ego.

Now you can say Thank God, now I understand what I am doing wrong, what I am dealing with. I live too much in my head! *And I say,* Well, get out of there. *You ask,* Well, how do I do that? *I answer,* Use my recording, and if you don't have the money, I will give it to you for nothing—if you are not too proud to accept a gift.

But where do you live if you don't live in your head?

If you don't live in your imagination, then you live in the light of reality. There is no other place. As soon as you live in the present moment—not in the past or future, but in the light of reality—then there is a new input, a new knowledge that replenishes and renews your spirit and body. As soon as your subconscious mind amplifies and dramatizes that input, lo and behold, you have a kingdom of heaven on earth within you and round about you. Jesus said that the kingdom of heaven is within you and around you, but men do not see it. Are you too busy seeing yourself as something you are not? Lost in the excitement of your imagination, you are king on a throne being worshiped; but in the light, you are a lowly dog being eaten alive.

About two years ago I dropped acid. About a year and a half ago, I freaked out. I had done some peyote in the meantime. I started your meditation, worked with it a little, and I've gotten into it. Things come out of me. I think I have been on a trip, you know, from being on acid, for about two years.

Let's go through what I said to the other man again. I see you have not grasped what I said. What are you trying to accomplish by taking drugs?

I was trying to understand all this.

No! You were trying not to understand. What you do want to understand is that you are God. You are still using a chemical "apple," trying to maintain a high. Your pride, like Adam's was, is still involved in escaping the truth to imagine that you are something you are not and never can be. You are a stubborn fool, seeking the reassurance of devils. You were trying to see yourself as infallible—always right, never wrong. Dope is hell's offering to this prideful need. Dope produces a trauma of escape. Prideful growth excites your mind, drawing your

75

guilty ego away from realizing how wrong you are. It is a very dangerous thing, indeed. Drugs are the same as the forbidden fruit of glory through knowledge, as original as Original Sin.

Every time you become high, you actually reinforce the sin that lost Paradise. Adam wanted to be God. The Tree of Knowledge of Good and Evil was a mind-freeing, mind-expanding shock, a trauma-producing poison. Every time you reach for a drug, you are reinforcing all the delusions of pride and crossing ever lower forbidden thresholds, thresholds to lower levels of mortal existence and to new lows of Satanic subservience.

I don't do drugs anymore. I refused! I am not going to!

But you are there now in the dungeon of your flesh, not far from hell. Unless you realize the truth and deal properly with what has happened to you through the use of drugs, you are bound to gravitate to other forms of escape. If you are not escaping, you will be forced to bear the pain of understanding before you are ready. If you are not reaching toward the light, then you are bound to reach away from the light. Reaching away represents a selfish love of the evil, of ego support, and that is the meaning of addiction.

Yes, I did fight back my conscience. I realize that.

You fought back your conscience as if there were something wrong with it and something right with you. That was the prideful implication behind the drug abuse, right?

Yes, I think so.

They are one and the same thing

I just realized that today, and it disturbed me.

Your conscience is really your salvation—"the good guy." But in your sin, conscience feels like "the bad guy."

76

In your wrong state of mind, right seems wrong and wrong becomes beautiful, alluring, and attractive.

If you love the truth, then you see by its light and it becomes your friend. It sustains you in humility and in truth. But if you hate the truth, then truth will become an enemy. The lie that exists for your glory draws you away into a velvet darkness and envelops you in the good feeling of a soul escaping in its own evolving flesh. The whole world is systematically controlled by this principle; the entire world is addicted to evil impulses. No wonder Satan is so plump!

We can bring down this wicked system simply by understanding what it is to become perfect. Being perfect is much easier on you than being imperfect. The more you escape, the more there is to run from. The more you face reality, the less reason you have to run. Going the right way, your conscience is your friend, helping you to overcome the loving infections of evil. The other way, evil is your friend, helping you to overcome good. It is embarrassing—and tough—at first, to face reality; but once you do, once the spell is broken, the cruel pressures of life will be easier to deal with. Then you won't need to cope with guilt by driving away your conscience and dredging up hell as a friend.

When I meditate, there has been a darkness where my third eye should be.

The difference between truth and evil is the difference between light and darkness. One word is synonymous with the other: evil = darkness, truth = light. Truth = Light = Life. Evil = Darkness = Death. They extend from one another, for better or for worse.

CHAPTER 6   Weakedness

There is a lot of talk about identity crisis in modern psychology, talk of the importance of establishing a good self-image, of developing a sense of personal worth. We are told that this can be done by looking outside ourselves for external reinforcement and support. But when you seek this *support* of yourself as you are instead of seeking the *truth* about yourself, you come down to an emotional, subconscious existence, separated from the substance of wisdom and discernment that God gave you to aid in your search for truth and true meaning.

The problem, very simply, is that you look for love, approval, meaning, identity, in every place except where it is to be found—within. Your attachments to men and machines exist in place of the proper attachment to truth and right. By appealing to your ego, Satan offers himself as a surrogate *god*, hoping by deception to lead you away from true light and Salvation. You become susceptible to his ploys, responding without awareness to his suggestions and teases. You learn to *feel* right by identifying with those things which seem right rather than learning to *be* right by obeying the light that is inside each of us.

79

Your entire self-image is based on words (and symbols) that produce feelings, and feelings which generate more (dependence on) words. This *externally based identity* exists through your low level of consciousness, and it is the common factor in all your involvements with people, places, and things. You are so emotionally identified with, and blinded by, words that you can no longer distinguish reality from illusion; thus you are not aware of your own spiritual decline and physical degeneration.

Do you see how identifying with beauty can imbue you with a false sense of being beautiful? Identify with religion, and you derive a feeling of being holy, of being saved, but what you really have is only the *illusion* of salvation. If you accept that deception, it will lead you further from truth, and you will need the distraction of new sins to help you escape the pains that grow when you see the pit into which you've fallen.

You may use the activity of resentment to escape the guilt, as though the thing of beauty, or even God himself, had suckered you into believing a lie. Of course, by believing in your false innocence, you perpetuate the guilt that began when you first rejected truth in favor of illusion. You lock yourself in more tightly to the hypnotic cycle of identification, feeling ever more guilty for escaping (again) into a lie and then needing more lies to diminish your awareness of the new guilt. You are caught in a compulsive, hypnotic pattern of dying, as though it were living.

The *high and mighty* wicked nature that grows from this cycle projects to friends and loved ones, confusing them and turning them into foes. Your family either identifies or becomes alienated, their wounded pride challenged by you to *get even*. So, you set into motion an evolution of intrigue and subtle revenge that can become incredibly complicated. You can easily compel your family to hurt you without their meaning to and then use the wounds they've inflicted to justify your continued cruelty to them and your sick way of life.

Consider the principle of martyrdom, a way of living in illusion in which one person or a group of people (spouse, family) is set up to appear to others in the worst possible light so that the one acting as martyr can seem comparatively noble and righteous. Take the classic case of a wife who, in seeking power, gathers support from strangers and friends against a seemingly cruel, angry, violent, drunken brute of a husband. If the martyr principle is at work and the truth be known, he may not be all that bad—he may be foolish, perhaps.

Possibly, the wife had a father she hated and she grew up needing a male object of judgment to stay ahead of the guilt that started with judging her father. Unconsciously she set her husband up as an object of hatred, to feed her corrupted pride by comparison. No matter what he did, he could never please her. For that reason, he became upset and lost what remained of his manly authority over her. When he tried to regain it, he did so in the only way he knew, the only way left—through sheer animal force, violence. Seeing just the surface of things, people felt sympathy for the poor woman and so were moved to help the wrong person. The wife, driven to fill a selfish, prideful need, conspired (unconsciously perhaps) to create a tyrant who would later become her victim, to satisfy her dual need for judgment and sympathy.

While this sort of thing can happen quite unconsciously, it could also be a deliberate use of the female's inherited power to confound and to control through confusion. You see, a man's understanding needs to be confounded before he can experience pride or lust, but it is through these that he is eventually controlled.

Extremely egotistical women are compelled to cripple and emasculate their husbands. The exciting and tempting confusion arouses lust in a man and drives him wild with desire. Deceitful and supportive *love* awakens pride in a man, but it also weakens him as he comes down to accept it. Once he has partaken of forbidden glory, he is bound to experience the other face of a woman, a hell that is visible only to her victims, because she presents an entirely different visage for the seduction of others.

While the husband is at work, the wife quietly undermines his authority, crippling and spoiling the children to possess their love. When he comes home at night after a hard day of work, he has rebellion on his hands. Now he is tempted to use more force than is necessary to bring about order in the home. Naturally, there is more rebellion against him, with the children forced to *take refuge* in mother—and there is the problem! Eventually dad becomes so frustrated and violent that the children are obliged to cling more closely to mother, seeking shelter in her from the enraged father.

Alas, by getting too close to mother (through rejecting the father's authority), the children become female-fixated and identified, especially the boys. The girls embody the mother's poison, and the boys grow up to be men who need that poisonous love, future victims of women from similar homes. In extreme cases, the boys may exchange identities with the mother, becoming so dominated by—and fixated to—the strength of the female that their male qualities are destroyed before being allowed to develop.

To repeat the principle: In order to gain power in her home, all the woman had to do was to act out the loyal, loving wife to her husband's face. When his back was turned, she permissively set the children against father by spoiling their egos rotten to need her protection and seductive love. She projected *her* wickedness onto the man, and it was that which everyone observed in him. She had literally stolen the *goodness* and the authority from the man.

To the untutored eye, the woman is the victim. Actually, the children are the real victims of mother's power to deceive. Putting on a long face, she obtains the faith and support of those around her. At the divorce court, the judge and jury are also deceived and bring an unjust judgment against a very frustrated man. Headlines often read *Man Shoots Wife and Children and Turns Gun on Self*. Now you know how the devil has done his work through the woman.

An important point should be made here. The condition that I have been describing *is not inevitable,* but is the result of choices made by both the man and the woman. Although each *contributes* to the other's devolution, one cannot be held ultimately responsible for the other. If either of them yearned to stop playing their mutually destructive game and desired nothing above seeing and understanding the truth about themselves, they would open the way for light and understanding to reach them. Every person is given the ability to change—all that is necessary is the deep, real desire to see the truth instead of the illusion. This is the gift that God has given us through the sacrifice of his son, Jesus Christ.

Remember that *things are not always what they seem*. It is easier to believe the devil than to recognize the truth.

People unconsciously side with the wrong person, because wrong people are always somehow more supportive and convincing; because they inherit the power to suggest and to deceive egos. God help little children!

Wicked people are "perfect" in their wickedness right from the start. They cannot make a *mistake*. Their actions are consistent with the direction they have chosen, so there is little or no resulting conflict to awaken them or to cause discomfort. They go on perfecting their beautiful wickedness, because no one knows how to stop them with love; because we all react with use, then with rebellion, and finally with resentment. The wicked cannot see their own wrong—everyone else is also wrong, so there is no *right* to serve as contrast. They suffer very little from pangs of conscience over what they do to you. Their wrongs appear right to them, because wrong is powerful, and it works for them. It is so easy to be wicked, powerful, and *perfect* in sin. You see, tease is the key to their power over every living being, and through tease, they refine an inherited wicked spirit that we fools employ.

Now let us see what sequence of events arises in your mind when you need love and are rejected. Rejection can tempt you to hate. That, in turn, makes you feel guilty. Resentment, being an inferior reaction, creates the feeling of unworthiness. What is your solution? You compensate for what you are not inside; you *act* perfect in order to be worthy of "love." That love, that approval of you as you are—if and when it comes—only makes you more wrong inside, by reinforcing the compulsion to pretend goodness to be worthy of receiving more love from admiring supporters (like a king).

Like it or not, you grow up serving for the approval of people (the tease of love), seething with secret resentment, because accepted or rejected, your *ego* problem compounds. You become a *Mr. Perfect* or an innocent *Miss Goody Two Shoes* to keep your spouse, parents, or others from being cruel or criticizing you. Not knowing how to deal with rejection or parental rage and condemnation, your ego pretends to be what it is not, and if you are *lucky*, you are rewarded with a Brownie button of (lie) *love*. You dare not be your real self—but then *no one wants you to be real*.

People can always use or tolerate phony goodness. It is easier to use a rotten person or a phony one than to be embarrassed by someone who possesses true awareness and goodness. (A truly honest and good person does not take advantage of others and, therefore, cannot be manipulated or taken advantage of.)

You grow up to be a people-pleasing phony. You feel frustration but stay ahead of your conscience by looking to do more pleasing and panhandling for more approval. You go on involving yourself more deeply in the mold in which you were cast, not knowing how to stop, perhaps afraid to stop. Alas, all your *perfect* behavior makes you very imperfect inside, which has an imperfect effect on your family. Your husband can be made to feel unworthy in comparison to your apparent—but phony—goodness. Off he goes to another woman for reassurance.

Ladies, falsely loving and being loved by the wrong in others will always reinforce the wrong in you, even as your catering brings out the beast in your husband. That beast is what projects from you, and it is what you judge in him. You may feel threatened and resentful because your *great goodness* has failed to reflect in your beloved. Worse, you can discover that you are a slave of a Frankenstein and all your beautiful efforts have been in vain!

God help you who marry if you must trade favors and compromise yourselves to make a beast *happy*. You can't allow him to be upset, for fear of losing the approval you need from him, carrying with it, as it goes, its message of "goodness." So, you spoil him rotten. Any displeasure he feels, you feel, and it pulls the rug from under your false sense of security, the fantasy that your *self-sacrifice* has been earning you.

Here, again, you can make your ego feel better by converting its cowardly *weakedness* into a *worth*. Your conditioning has made you a psychotic slave with a false sense of purpose—you are a *peacemaker*. It is a weakness, of course, but you see it as love and goodness, and your sense of worth comes down to depend on keeping peace through appeasement. Giving in to evil makes you appear to be a good and self-sacrificing fool, but eventually you become a martyr for *righteousness*. The nicer you are, the more that becomes a temptation which spoils your husband and children. Naturally, a part of them likes it and leads you on. For a while you think you are in control, but the next moment you are pummeled into the ground.

When your husband and children sense that the game you are playing is cultivating their bad side for your private pleasure, judgment, and use, they may use you and your *weakedness* and harbor contempt for your *kindness*. They may sense that your apparent kindness is hurting them, bringing out their wickedness to serve you in some mysterious way. In that case, if they don't turn around and *outfake your goodness*, they become more

86

and more cruel to punish you or to stop you from being so wickedly kind. Then you turn around and interpret that as a lack of appreciation caused by not being kind enough! You will feel that their failing is due to love's failing.

Responding in panic, you become ever *kinder*. Responding in rage, they are only trying to stop your wicked kindness from destroying them completely. A violent man will even act to disfigure and disable his wife's beauty and sensuality in an attempt to destroy the power that they wield over his spirit.

You can confound yourself with notions and ideas arising that were never suggested by anyone. You figure things out wrongly and blame your problems on wrong causes. Inferiority and bodily self-consciousness might cause you to associate the problem with a part of your anatomy—a common misidentification. You may take an imperfect part of you, such as your nose, and blame that for your unhappiness or curse God for the deformity. Your cure becomes a complete distraction from what the problem really is—*you*! So, you get worse. If plastic surgery makes you look beautiful, you only use that beauty in a way which makes you more ugly inside.

Your mind can become completely preoccupied with finding answers—nevertheless wrong ones. Frustration and blame make you depressed and morbid. The morbid, hopeless feelings draw negative suggestions (thoughts) of death, and they, in turn, begin to motivate you to externally destructive, and self-destructive, acts.

When you have deteriorated sufficiently and moved close enough to hell in spirit, you can even hear Satan, the author of your suffering, speaking to you in voices.

He says, *Kill yourself: you will be free, and you will find peace.*

Will you believe him now that you have heard this message of truth?

CHAPTER 7

The Dark Side of Love

When someone says "I need you," does that mean "I love you"? If sex, or need, is love, then is it true that the more need you have, the more love there is? Surely that implies a growing dependency, a loss of freedom. And if love is supposed to come from people, yet it is something we all need and lack, then how can anyone provide it to another?

The answer, obviously, is that no one can. What you see passing for *love* is nothing more than need and a need to be needed, with one party pretending to fulfill the need of the other in order to satisfy his own need. It's a con game.

Our lives are confounded and our minds manipulated by imparting the wrong meanings to words. No doubt, you've heard the expression *I love too much, that's what's the matter with me*; but look carefully at that statement. Surely in true love there is the perfect balance in everything. If this is so, how can love possibly do anything in excess? Where is the contradiction?

What people really mean is that they *use* and *need* too much and, for the sake of what they need, allow themselves to be used and abused. Maybe you give your all under pressure and call your weakness love. A growing ego need to be stroked tends to make you supportive and spoils people to take advantage of you. *Weakness brings out cruelty in others, to which you must surrender your substance to keep the peace.* Unfortunately, that kind of giving or loving cannot work, as it is nothing more than a vampire-zombie relationship.

The trouble is that we usually associate need with something good. We think the same of those who give in to, or gratify, our needs. What we are *really* looking at here is a *dark love*, a strange compulsion of something in us to fulfill or to be fulfilled by kindred types.

The relationship between a creator and his creatures happens to be one of need. When corruption enters to displace our true Creator, the corrupter becomes the re-creator of our identity. Now the re-creator must be supportive of his creation, which is to say, he must answer the need of his creation; otherwise they would cease to exist, and he could not love through them.

However, this support can be viewed in two ways—either as being a service to the creature purely or a worship of, and for, the re-creator *by* the creature in exchange for that life-giving support—in other words, as the creator being worshiped by the creature or as the creator worshiping (supporting) the creature.

Looking at it from one point of view, it can seem as though the creator is actually serving his creature. A corrupted person can look upon his supportive creator as a lesser being serving his pride and not see his own servitude for the sake of that fulfillment, which is (of course) the only thing the seducer-*re-creator* sees. The victim views the seducer as a lover supporting his kingsize ego.

In reality, the re-creator feeds the deception that manifests itself in the corrupted as a need for re-creator reinforcement (support). That growing need for the re-creator fulfills the corrupted's own vampirish need to be needed—a demigodlike role. While the true (invisible) God rewards our need for truth with life, the false god of clay does the opposite. He steals that life with lies, draining and crippling his creature into greater need. Paradoxically, the victim is only too happy to experience this need, because the corruption that he craves is like a creation of his ego; it makes him feel loved, fulfilled, safe in his corrupted form.

The politics of tyranny always reward weakness with a Brownie button of approval, calling it goodness; and then to the wicked (those most like themselves), they may give dominion over the weak.

There is always an affinity (which passes for love) for anyone or anything that supports your growing greed needs. You can lust after food, dope, drink, horse racing, or wild, wild women as though it were loving. Do you see how many shades of (wrong) meaning there are for love?

For better or for worse, love is always a mystical fulfillment that is difficult to comprehend. Psychotics have a sick craving for the *fulfilling* love of their supportive *creator-type* vampires. However, if we are yearning for the truth to fulfill our souls, to correct us from those corrupt cravings, then in a very special place in our hearts we will find what we have been seeking; we shall awaken one morning spiritually incompatible with worldly love. We will then see what is wrong with our selfish needing.

We have confused everyone, including ourselves, by seeming to be nice, good, dutiful, and loving, when in fact we are not. Our niceness, far from being love, is only a performance to obligate others to accept us in some way. The sweet face we put on, the kind deeds we do to get approval, are designed to tempt others to respond to our secret unhealthy needs. Therefore, being nice and being patronizing are generally *not* loving, but forms of prideful selfishness and ways of manipulating someone's mind and feelings.

If you are playing this game, you are dependent as a creator and as a creature and dare not speak up and be yourself. Honesty would have a devastating effect. As soon as you are honest and tell the truth, the friend you were supporting (to get him to support you) immediately becomes an adversary.

All phony niceness is cruel, because it strokes the fault and uses it to feed that secret need, destroying and sowing confusion in the process. Sensing that cruelty, we experience rebellion and contempt. Rebellion against a creator, based on hostility, sets the victim creature on one of two paths, each leading to its own tragic chain of events.

PATH 1. Resentment that leads to guilt ends in conformity. Here you become emotionally too *close* to the re-creator, obliged to contribute to his illusion of worth and power for the sake of your own security. This makes you, the creature, dependent on the practice of a degrading worship that you see as an ennobling service, in order to hold on to your *security*. In your subconscious mind the worship is designed to compel the corrupter to service *your* illusions and complete in you the only identity you know—that which you believe to be your own but is really the corrupter's.

As you are used and wasted, you sense your sin in terms of a growing anxiety and guilt. It is possible to stay ahead of this guilt for a while by giving more of yourself and of the degrading sacrifices, surrendering yourself more completely (to be complete) to the *glorious and glorifying* source of your corruption. At best, this is a feeble attempt to identify with greatness, for all you are and ever will be is *them*.

Imagine setting someone up as a god in order to *become* him. This may sound a little far out, but it is the only way to be anything when you are a psychotic. Incidentally, fluctuating between being mean and being kind keeps a victim angry, off balance, guilty, and confused, enhancing the effect of the creator-corrupter's "goodness" by intensifying the victim's love involvement with something "good." That is what is called a love-hate relationship.

PATH 2. If the victim has any real spirit, he rebels, pulling the rug out from underneath the creator-corrupter's pride so that his vampirish vital *soul food* is lost. At this point, another manipulator usually rushes in to take advantage of the victim's rebellious spirit. Seeing the loss of his victim, the original creator-corrupter deceives himself by believing (the lie) that the troubles are due to not *loving* (corrupting) enough and, so, is challenged to try harder, to compete, to seduce more. Motivated by rejection and rage, *god* now tries harder to outmaneuver the rival *god* by giving more sex, money, or personal favors—anything to retrieve the loyalty and dependence of the victim.

Unfortunately, such pursuit and prostitution only reveal use, not love. This is the very thing that the victim despises in the corrupter, driving him further away, usually to someone far "*less worthy*."

93

A god without a subject is all alone—frightened, upset, and confused. If you are the corrupter-*re-creator*, you cannot understand why your *beloved* is faithful to worthless scoundrels after you were so *loving* and "good." You resent your victim for not needing you anymore; you could even resent him for *dying*.

What you are looking at now is jealousy—a dependent, possessive emotion that you consider to be one of the many aspects of love. *You need your victim's dependency, for only through that symbiosis can you get close enough to feed on another's soul.* Oh, what terrible things are *need* and the *need to be needed!*

The guilt behind a corrupter's love need is exposed when he loses a soul. Instead of looking at the selfishness that drove away the object of love, he gazes more intently at the other person's betrayal, seeing it at first with rage, then with guilt and a greater longing to possess. (This longing is called jealousy.) Jealousy, masquerading as love, disguises and justifies the sinful need that you call love. Can you see how the tyrant and victim can become addicted to each other, unable to function without a feeding partner?

Closeness passing for love is a perfect blending of "weakedness" and wickedness. The weak have a weakness for the wicked, as do the wicked for the weak. Mortal love is nothing more than a pejorative emotional affinity of two sick souls. Remember, the corrupted conveniently sees his creator as a servant—and the *pusher* views his *pushover* with contempt, considering him fair game.

What confounds everything in this kind of relationship is the resentment that festers and clouds the true issue. You see, just as long as you falsely believe that your craven need to use or to be used is love, you are bound to continue betraying and being betrayed.

Underneath any resentment is guilt, from which rises the need for a more intensified love (support).

It could be that this abnormal craving began with rejection, which caused terrible guilt through the subsequent sin of resentment. It is at this point that the soul tries to redeem itself from a sin of judgment by seeking to feel good and acceptable, by prostrating itself before the judged. This prideful need causes us to sell ourselves for human approval. The idea or motive is to manipulate a creator-corrupter to soothe guilt and stroke those childish ego needs.

Man comes into this world with a need to *love*. His egocentrism confuses that with a divine *right* to use. Woman inherits the counterpart, a need to be needed that lets itself be used in order to get what it needs from the man.

Here, then, is the pleasure of use and of using the user, passing for love—the classic coupling of two selfish spirits. When harm appears, each blames the other and tries to assert independence by running to another lover, another ego support system. Judgment and resentment will, *without fail*, translate to guilt, which manifests itself as a growing need to love or to be loved, in an attempt to restore to the soul what was lost through resentment. This is what makes us prostitute ourselves for the approval of others.

It is not unusual for a love-hungry parent to be threatened by the love needs of a child. That is where rejection often begins, leading to a resentment-based hunger and the endless, futile search for the corrupter-creator's "love."

CHAPTER 8

How to Destroy a Perfectly Bad Relationship

The false concept of female devotion—the woman's traditional role of catering to men—is addictive to man, just as the concept of male lust, which is stirred up by that role playing, is addictive to woman. When the female supports the male's weakness in order to obligate him to serve her selfish ends, she eventually experiences the result of her *love* in terms of frustration and betrayal. Through her use of man's weakness (his ego), she weakens him further.

This leaves him susceptible to the same temptation she offers when it is presented from other sources, so that frustration and betrayal become the result of her supportive *love* (use). For women, gratification is more an ego-mental experience than a physical one, while for men it is mostly a physical event. Either way, selfishly cultivated gratification leads to guilt, frustration, and resentment, which amplify the need for frustrating "love." It is a vicious cycle.

The driving ambition for human love like any ambition, is a madness of the soul, and just as long as we think of it as our divine due, we will continue selling ourselves down the river for it, reaping a continuous harvest of frustration.

You are free from this cycle the moment you are glad to realize that your need for love is just another variation of the folly of pride. The light of understanding will, in that very moment, release you from having to do anything more for *love*. No longer are you anyone's slave, and never again will you have to feel resentment in being denied *love* or feel frustration because your need was used.

The reader would no doubt think the writer mad were it not for a latent recognition of, or some personal experience with, this universal principle of sin.

The false need to love and to be loved is related to ancient pride, a guilt that the entire human race shares in its heritage, a *crime scene* to which every male must return in order to find one of two things—either *redemption* (salvation from the cycle) or *ego gratification* (business as usual). Until the mystery of finding love (a life reinforcement) from the proper source (God) is unraveled, we all continue to suffer from *business as usual*, a syndrome of two selfish people coming together in ignorance, compounding the suffering of the original sin.

Original Sin was (and still is) use by way of failure to love correctly, becoming a greater need to use that passes for ever greater love.

Ambition (to become God) is the name of the sin of pride, as was pointed out earlier in the text. To perpetuate man's illusion of himself as a king—a deity—he needs a subject to dominate, to use for worship. His subject offers support, to which the "king" becomes addicted. Eventually the subject turns the tables and becomes the ruler of the stupid, selfishly motivated king.

Pride will not or can not correct (love) another person of the very quality it needs to use.

A woman knows when a man is looking at her with longing, like a hungry animal. It is the way in which men look that mystically endows the woman with an uglifying energy, a power to effect a devolution in the man by making him proud of his failing while destroying (and re-creating) his spirit. That longing look, when met with a body language of approval, emotionally involves the man, while stirring up the carnal feelings which his ego associates with life.

A sizzling steak or a piece of strawberry shortcake can arouse desire in you even though your body may not need food. If you are guilty or bored, the morsel can become even more appealing and can engage your attention in that same special way, creating in you a longing which you associate with discovering love.

Because of the man's original default and resulting sexual abuse, and because of the power that mother now has over the children, every boy grows up with a woman's nature inside him. This female-centered nature, which grew from the seduction of the woman and was born from her, must return to its source to reseed itself and to perpetuate its ego existence.

This is the heart of man's need. As he reaches physical maturity, he tries to escape that founding and dominating spirit, only to find it again in another form—an apparently friendly and ego-supportive wife. Thus, full circle—here we are back at the original scene of the crime. Just as a seed doesn't fall far from its tree, so the ego of man cannot go far without the support of the spirit of its creator.

Here we see the reason why father fell in need of (not in love with) mother, who unconsciously and selfishly cultivated his weakness just as though she were loving him, begetting still another generation of users.

To use is to die through the object of use, to give it an awesome power to alter and manipulate the user. The evolution of selfhood, of change and decay, relays life and death through this use called *love*, which is what sin and death are all about.

Therefore must man find the higher order of love if he wants to transcend all his slavish needs. To accomplish that, his perception of life and of love must change. *To overcome the woman within, he must find the way to correct (love) the supportive woman god without. Experience proves the kind of love you have.*

There is another reason men idolize women. By holding her up on a sexual pedestal, man can enter into sin and lose himself in it completely, identifying with the lover of his failing as though it were a glorious thing. The corrupted always idolize their corrupter so that they can avoid the awareness of what sin and love have done to them, all the while emulating and becoming the god they have created. Any way you slice it, for better or for worse, "love" is a reaction that involves or immerses you in a process of becoming what you love.

Notice the difference between the need *to* love and the need *for* love. The need for (female) love is a (selfish) childish need. It is a carryover from an ancient ambition, a yearning for the woman identity in man to complete itself to a vainglorious promise held up by a woman outside of him. Carried to an extreme, a man can lose his humanity completely and devolve into bestiality and homosexuality. Once begun, this process of woman-based devolution continues to the grave.

After a man has been corrupted—let us say *changed*—into a criminal, he needs criminal types to complement and to reassure him. Where stealing was once a crime, it now becomes a virtue, something he has to be proud of to avoid the shame of it. A man who's been emasculated and corrupted by a woman becomes dependent on her seduction as a diversion from the awareness of his failing. By the same token, a woman who makes a monkey of a man re-creates an animal dependent on what created it.

We come back now to that definition of *need* as "love." Whenever there is something wrong (inside), this need affinity exists in one form or another. The cry of a displaced, sick, embryonic self ripples out as a distress signal to the trauma source. Quite often it is a desperate and violent demand, manipulating or compelling the source to rise to the occasion of the need like a *hell's angel*.

Here is the principal reason why female love produces such pathetic, dependent, contemptible, psychotic, schizophrenic, irresponsible creatures. It is not really the fault of woman, because as I said earlier, man should be the one who does the loving and correcting rather than cultivating her to *love* him. His selfish pride will never correct the guileful, lying qualities that his ego craves to exist, for which he adventures through the debasement of woman's soul to some elusive idea of glory. This holds true of every corrupting and sustaining influence imaginable—drugs, alcohol, gambling, music, and so on.

Man ought to communicate a correcting love to woman, which is to say, he should oppose the guile he selfishly needs. Instead, he teaches her carnal knowledge to support his selfish pride. For this reason, one need not fear temptation—for it rises mostly to a selfish call. A person is tempted *only* by his own wickedness.

Temptation has no power except what you give to it. Therefore, *repent! Stop using!* Cease blaming and hating, because blaming is another use of our beloved that also gives evil its power to enslave.

Female pride feels excitement not only in the presence of male weakness, but also with children and grandchildren. Often the female ego is challenged by the opportunity to redeem itself from the failure of past love-hate relationships. A female's demon is awakened, called up, by a victim's feebleness and need, to relive its life through men and little children—as a god is supposed to live through its creatures. A spoiled, rebellious, degenerate, vile, and violent slob usually emerges from woman's love—a terrible blow to her pride and sense of goodness. Angry and threatened, she faces a choice of either *loving* (seducing) more to prove her worthiness or of dumping the unsatisfactory (depleted) victim and focusing on another fool.

There is, for a woman, an almost irresistible excitement in living through and dominating something animal. There is, also, for foolish men, an irresistible need for the supportive, redeeming love of a (wrong) woman. As you can see, a woman's love redeems only in the sense that it distracts man from the awareness of his pitiful condition and boosts his hope of glory in pride and dreams, *robbing him of repentance*, reducing him to the state of a violent dog or a whimpering puppy.

A woman must be gotten out of her husband or son, otherwise the saving love of God cannot get in. You see, the woman's love displaces God's love. The two cannot coexist.

Taking upon herself the responsibility to save another person (which is the male role) can drive a woman mad, because by trying to save, she actually worsens the victim's condition, while becoming more sick and confused herself. She cannot possibly succeed in her attempt, because she is motivated by a selfish desire for personal glory or self-salvation. It is not the responsibility of any mortal being to be the savior of another—only God has that power, through our (correct) acceptance of, and belief in, Jesus Christ as His son and spokesman.

The guilt of trying to be a savior translates to strong feelings of responsibility. And there is a flicker of truth in that feeling, but it is *only for the guilt of being tricked into proudly picking up that responsibility for loving*. If she could view her role in the proper light, she would be free of the compulsion to play God and savior. Her pride turns the truth around, as if to say *You are selfish for rebelling and not fulfilling your* loving *duty*. This is the false and ancient belief that drives a woman (resentfully) to continue trying to save the man.

Adam blamed Eve for his own failing and most likely succeeded in making her feel guilty and responsible for his sin as well as for her own. Ever since then, contemporary Adam has been able to make contemporary Eve feel responsible for the rest of his failings. Do you see how a little bit of truth, viewed in a partial light, is enough to make her accept *all* the blame, so that she keeps taking the blame for her children's faults as well, robbing them of repentance and change?

The whole truth is that man's wicked need placed the woman in the position of catering to it, and *that is precisely why he always falls short of true manliness*. He fails and then falls and blames her. She resents him, which amplifies the sense of blame; then she begins *loving* (catering) to make up to him for her "failure." On the surface, it seems to him as though she truly is responsible for what is happening to him.

You are gazing now at the root cause of the suffering of the entire human race. The harder a woman tries to help her man, the worse he becomes, because her love can never be anything more than a seduction, a support that she has been tricked into giving to the man. The result of her misguided support is a miserable, pathetic, or even violent wretch who can do nothing except blame her (again) and continue to cry out for what she cannot possibly give.

Dear ladies, I do have compassion for you. As a man, I want you to know the real truth about men. But are *you* ready to see it? Perhaps you enjoy reveling in judgment of his weakness and lust.

To repeat the theme once more: *Man's first guilt is in using, the second guilt, in laying responsibility for his use on the woman's shoulders. The woman's guilt is in believing she is completely responsible and trying resentfully to redeem her "mistake" by saving the man.*

The guilty frustration that every woman feels is amplified by the terrible contempt which she has for a man's weakness. Such resentment has two facets: resentment of the man for not responding to her "loving" treatment (doctors often blame their patients for not getting well rather than question their treatment) or resentment of his failure to correct her, to understand what it is that she truly needs and wants.

It is man's destiny to make woman over in a right way. Instead, he uses her in her ignorance and confusion;

so she makes him worse. Here is a modern Adam joined again to the wrong in Eve, with one slight difference from the first pair—they do not commit an original sin but merely reinforce, in ignorance, the old one.

So it is that man, with his psychic need demanding an ego-reinforcing love, sustains the world in its present state of misery.

Now that you have a different view of love, can yours ever be the same?

CHAPTER 9

Sexperience

Whenever you put someone on a pedestal, you give that person the power to suggest to you that which is not true, that which you want to believe.

Once you have handed over this power, your nature becomes altered by the effect the lie has on you. To your horror, you find that you cannot take the power back again, that you need a deceitful presence in order to survive. You are now under a spell, a compulsion.

We all need someone to inspire the forbidden way, to suggest that wrong is right, and to assuage our guilt. Without our amiable rogues, we would suffer from too much awareness. It is only natural to feel stricken with guilt and to climb the walls from withdrawal when we give up or lose our favorite poison person.

The people who seduce us with suggestion also "save" us with suggestion. Just so long as you continue in pride and selfishness, that long will you give others the power to suggest your dream existence. They will suggest drugs, alcohol, kinky sex; they will steal, cheat, and rob you; and you will go along for their approval, to relieve either past sins or new sins which require outside sanction.

Because of Original Sin, the human race is externalized; that is to say, we have lost the power to suggest to ourselves. That authority now belongs to others. We need external motivation to function (pridefully), and we need people to affirm a lie as truth.

Suggestions can be nonverbal. They can be implied and embodied. There is a body language. A smile contains a simple message, does it not?

Any professional hypnotist worth his salt knows how to transfer the "authority to command" to an object so that the presence of the object can act as a suggestion trigger. Amulets, flags, and religious symbols are among the many objects that can reinforce and inspire feeling and behavior patterns by their mere presence.

Perhaps the single most powerful object on earth is a woman's form. Any establishment that wishes to retain control must use the "woman effect" to keep masses of men as soft, malleable, mindless beasts of burden to the state. A beautiful woman embodies the serpent of culture; she is a statement of goodness, and to be embraced by her is, to a man, a sign of worthiness. Like a flag, she represents all the meaning and messages inherent in culture.

As it was in Paradise, so is it carried forward to this day, with the serpent of establishment using the female—first to disturb and then to maintain the established order (of hell) on earth.

Women unnaturally inherit the hypnotic attention of men, and attention is what is vital to the transmission of any suggestion. There can be very little learning or discovery without some kind of attention and excitement.

Once your soul has been seduced, your attention is no longer yours to give; it becomes the property of the seducer, permanently fixated to the source (of corruption). Experiment; hold your mind *still* if you can. Immediately your mind wanders. You begin to think of all sorts of distractions. If you are able to lock your attention to anything at all, it is because it has been captured by sex, greed, and worry. Man cannot free his mind from the grasp of its selfish memories and pursuits.

Can any man keep his mind off women for long? Any interest that draws a man's mind away from women merely leads it right back again. I say this because man is selfish and ambitious, traumatized from the day he is born to need female reassurance! Rarely for noble reasons does man wish to attain anything. There is usually but one motive, sometimes with different forms—desire for glory involving the support of a woman, or lust to buy all the glory-sustaining women one can with one's ill-gotten wealth.

Were you to purchase a '65 Chevrolet, you might become conscious of how many of those same cars were around, something you perhaps hadn't noticed before. The fixation of your ego onto your car increases your awareness of similar cars. In the same way, a heavy ego-fixation with a woman's sexual nature can cause a woman to become a man's god, so that everything begins to remind him of her sexuality. Everything that leads away from a fixation to woman will eventually bring it right back again to sex.

To survive, the pride of man must be continuously distracted away from reality through a reinforcing person who displaces God. The original fixation itself must be reinforced through more and more lie appeal and trauma with the source.

Why is this? you ask. It is because man's ego cannot bear to behold what he has become and what the future promises. Anything that is strong enough to pull a man's mind away from a woman is 1) suggested by the woman and 2) the cause of a sexual impulse which leads right back to her again.

Mortal man exists through a series of traumas. He needs intrigue to hold his attention away from the truth. His soul must be continuously baptized in excitement. And whatever that excitement is must, of necessity, be wrong, because the nature of pride can survive only through deeper wrong involvements.

The soul experiences embarrassment and friction the moment its attention is released from the excitement and the intrigue of sin. However, the trauma necessary to re-gain a man's attention brings out sexual desire. Violence can do it, as well as the attainment or the frustration of any goal. *Anything wrong is sexually exciting.*

To reiterate, the fixation of attention is not only a source of relief from knowledge of guilt, but it is also the focal point through which sensual man comes into exist-ence, sustained in a female base. The male fixation with the teasing woman is the invitation for the *she* self to enter with her commands to make man ambitious for her.

Now you may very well ask, why should man conform so easily to suggestion? The answer, in part, is the ques-tion *How can any creature refuse the demands of a god whom he needs in order to exist himself?*

There are a number of other factors which go together to imply that woman has become man's God, but man is unaware of what is happening, because his ego is *afraid* of being aware. Being unaware, he has nothing to counter all her subtle hypnotic influences upon his subconscious mind. In order to become less aware of truth about himself, *he must become more aware of her.* Mankind is asleep—awake only in his dreams.

All traumas tend to displace the original personality with something of the trauma source, and this new child of trauma (sin) exists in relationship to what created it, through a continuing love-hate relationship. So much is this so, that a man will soon realize he is nothing without a woman, just as he is nothing without God. That is something he would rather not know, so he avoids humiliation by burying himself more deeply in her.

So mankind is bound—locked mentally, emotionally, and physically—into womankind. He will bring the world to her for approval. He is so externally motivated that he needs female permission or support for what he selfishly wants.

This is why it is so hard for a man to believe in himself or to achieve anything without an exciting woman. His need can be so obsessive that it may become impossible to think of anything but women, to the exclusion of his goals. So great can this hunger be, that he must have sex to clear his mind; otherwise, he cannot function in the business world. The greater the guilt, the more the mind dwells on sex. Again he needs her, to get sex off his mind in order to get ahead. Even the excitement of a goal can take over the process of arousing lust.

Just as female pressure creates a sexual need, so does guilt create a need that naturally aligns itself with suggestions to drink, to smoke, and to take drugs. Woman was, and still is, the original "fixer," the source of man's fall and escape into being. The woman principle still holds true here, because drugs have power to suggest activities to get money to again obtain the "benefit" of the drugs. So the lust for women can become the lust for anything that will reduce awareness.

One tends to resist an obvious suggestion, but if we do listen to advice, the underlying motivation is usually selfish. We are simply hearing what we want to hear. We fall in love with people who have common interests, join clubs, and mingle with people with similar selfish fixations; and so we go on enjoying the dumb things we have, yet still want.

Remember, you are presently an externalized creature, incapable of responding to internal direction. Therefore, you crave the external tease. By necessity, you have to find a playmate who agrees with what you want, thereby justifying what you have already done and releasing you to achieve and to obtain more. But once you have obtained, you need a source to comfort you in your guilt. You literally will work your selfish self to death for a person who gives you permission to have what you want. The catch is that you must give up your authority to that person to keep from feeling guilty.

The abuse of anything—drugs, drink, or sex—as the use of women, represents a rejection of reality. The use of such things constitutes a new guilt the very moment it is a *salvation* from a former guilt. One can drink to forget the guilt of drinking, make love to forget the guilt of making love; yet the use of anything produces the very symptom from which you are escaping. Thus there is no escape from the addiction to sex save love—which comes through unselfishness.

The sexual aspect of the power to suggest is by no means confined to woman. It is possible to transfer sexual hysteria to just about anything.

Whatever massages an ego also brings out a sexual desire for itself. In a homosexual perversion, one person is fixated, enslaved, to the guile of the other. Alcohol and drugs are also female substitutes. As they tease, they release the victim from awareness of guilt, secretly reinforcing through sexuality all the ambitions of the soul.

As the tease factor releases the mind to achieve (and sin), it creates a (sexual) need to forget the guilt of those achievements.

Do you see how you are committed, conscripted, into the service of an evil power? Careful! The evil is not the *woman* herself, it is what the male ego need draws up through her by his rituals with her body.

Then, how, you wonder, can a man break the hypnotic spell over his mind? The answer is to become "ambitious" to know and to do what is *right*.

Surely you realize that what motivates you becomes your god. If you escape, you won't get far. Why? Because by psychic and physiological necessities, you will be drawn to the same spirit in another who, by the very act of accepting and loving you as you are, brings out sexual desires and enslaves you again. A man's need is a demand, and that need has its own unspoken command to woman, obliging her to play the ancient supporting role to help him play God.

What does one do with this need that teaches women to be witches? The love with which men love (sex) is the failing love, the falling away from what love is all about, deep in one's soul. The lust for woman is a displaced need for God. The woman—rather the spirit behind her—is presently the dominating and supporting principal force in the world. Remember that for man to aspire (pridefully), he must experience trauma with something wrong. He must give power to a woman or to a woman substitute to get motivation and then use her consolation to forget the guilt.

At best, man is a weak, phony, womanizing weasel. At worst, he is a violent devil. At best, he lets his wife ruin his kids, sitting like a rooster on a perch, as Mister "Nice Guy." He simply cannot oppose her, because of his selfish need. Defiled by her love, he becomes an impossible, spoiled, conceited, selfish, irresponsible, violent, and rebellious swine. The bigger his ego swells, the more women he needs to send messages to his ego, through the greater sin of infidelity. Anxiety and confusion are compounded by infidelity.

Is it possible to get between the suggestion and the suggesting source? Surely if one could get between Hitler and his soldiers, one could win a war without bloodshed. It is through man's use of woman that Hitlers rise and hell on earth begins, so how does one get between a man and a woman and her source of suggestion? The answer is true love, a selflessness that transcends the psychological use which is manifested in sexual abuse.

Any suggestion or pressure is one part of the circle, but the response to that suggestion is the whole circle. No response, no power to the source.

Consider the radio; it does not depend on signals to exist. A radio is still a radio without being turned on. But man is created (and re-created) out of signals—words. He can be turned on and tuned into the word of the Serpent or to the wordless Word deep in his heart.

Man is a word-created instrument, and as such, he expresses the spirit originating through the word as it is made flesh. The life of that instrument is based on responding to the same spirit thereafter. If your life has been changed by sin, you are naturally subject to additional negative suggestion. You start to believe the worst about others and lies about yourself and you become attracted to the worst in everyone.

The Bible tells us that Salvation comes by the Word, and the Word comes by hearing. The inwardly revealed Word of God is needed to cancel the incoming suggestions that reinforce the Serpent nature concealed in your nature. All the verbal truth in the world cannot change you unless you receive it in a special way, one through which awakening occurs. No, you cannot absorb words like a sponge and then preach to others. That is pride still eating of the Tree of Knowledge, without the benefit of understanding. The kind of belief you have and the lifestyle that grows from it hinge on a mysterious ability to receive the Word with a right attitude.

Are you presently confused? Do you feel the lust for religion pulling you in one way while your conscience draws you in another? Are the tease and pressures of life winning? They always will win until you know the way. That way can't be discovered until you have a true commitment to discover it. If you want what is right, then you will be able to hear and receive the true Word. You can be saved from Original Sin, the original hypnosis through which originated your hell on earth! Remember, as you sink lower, people, places, and things take on new suggestive (sexual) meanings. Each meaning that is dramatized debilitates you and sets you up to read deeper and darker (sexual) meanings into everything. No wonder you are depressed!

Every time you contemplate doing wrong, there is a sense of excitement that causes you to cross over a mental frontier to receive sin nature into your heart. After that you are bound to go on sexually reinforcing that nature as if you were being good to yourself.

Satan's method is to save you from one sin through the hope of another sin. The secret of true Salvation is not to trick people out of their various compulsive allegiances to wine, women, song, gambling—their petty Hitlers—because that would mean an external transference from one (sexual) tyrant-enslaver to another, like a monkey swinging from one branch to another with its prehensile tail. The spirit behind all those "salvations" remains constant, using different forms to trick your mind.

The secret of life lies in awakening souls by the inspired spoken word, which brings them back to the wordless Word in their own hearts. A person who does not respond to the pressure of suggestion reveals the Word of God to the adversary, and that shock can mean either devastation or Salvation. *That great shock literally gets between the person and his false beliefs—his secret source of wicked suggestion.*

As I have pointed out, every selfish being seeks a (false) sense of his own worth. By seeking a lie, he sets himself up for catalysts—lies and liars—that germinate in him a lifestyle which advances in a wrong direction, toward the growth of his rotten ego. No man is tempted except by his own *lust,* and when *lust* is conceived, it brings forth *sin.* When *sin matures,* it brings forth *death.*

Because of Original Sin, every man has a woman in him through his mother. Because of original corruption, every man lusts after the lie that originated him, but woman yearns for the love (of the father) that she has never known. Sadly, the terrible craving and demand that man has for woman blocks his light and perverts her true love so that it supports his beast.

It is the nature of woman to serve. She was created for that purpose only, but if she is compelled to serve the sickness in man, God help them both!

What beautiful friends men could have, were they only to know the obedience to the Creator and the love God would impart to them for their women! And women, seeing the nobility of men, would be drawn away from their private hells to join with the God of man. As it stands now, man has drawn away from the inner realm of Good to become a slave of sex, of death, and of hell.

Obedience is the key. Don't you see how suggestion is transmitted through obedience? Obedience is a response of the faithless to a lie and of the faithful to the truth.

Because of pride, man cannot transmit divine orders of caring love. His love is selfish, and woman gets the message of his using. Given time, woman can realize that her cooperation is creating a selfish, irresponsible beast. Some women shrink away in horror, because they know it is not right—it is not what they want out of men—while other, more wicked females revel in discovering their power over obedient fools.

It is a woman's good pleasure to respond to the suggestion of a responsible man and a child's pleasure to obey an obedient, respectful wife. It is a military chain of command with enlightened reason at the helm.

Ladies, if you have problems with your man, it is because you were attracted to his weakness by your own

117

compatible wickedness. What you never learned about life you have now discovered through *sex-perience.*

Because of that original cause (still with you), Paradise was lost. Your Garden of Eden is now a jungle in hell.

Your future hinges on your willingness to do what is right. Even though doing right may cause a woman to lose all the (false) security that she has built up, the devotion and power which come to her from a man are nothing more than his response to her for playing the devil's advocate to him. She is doomed to lowering herself forever if she tries to stay ahead of his need for her to serve tease, excitement, and trauma. A sick man needs newer, more exciting thresholds to venture across and to grow; otherwise, he becomes threatened (by his conscience), restless, and bored. Denied, he will feel betrayed. (Actually, he discovers the betrayal of the woman's false love.) So it comes to pass that he demands kinky, tricky sex to provide for that sense of adventure and growth.

You can literally feel yourself sinking as hell rises through you, its evidence in your power to suggest. You can feel your man calling up a dark spirit in you to serve his wickedness. You will see that it is not you whom he loves, it is not you he really worships, but it is a terrible spirit rising up through your ravaged body, and you are no longer in control.

As long as you, dear lady, are ambitious and prideful, you can distort the meaning of those devotions. You can drown yourself, your sorrows, and your insecurities in his dying to your "glory." You will have longing for the love you want and loathing for the power you get. You serve only to become corrupted by, and addicted to, power.

Do you want to be free? Then realize the divine folly of pride. That, alone, will begin to change the course of your life. You'll not be able to go along with what you did before you became aware of the truth, and you'll find yourself no longer bound by the old ways. Don't doubt what you see now. Don't let yourself be persuaded or pressured back to the old ways, no matter what happens. Now you know what is right in your heart. Cleave to it. Only that commitment will separate you from hell.

Disarm yourself by revealing to your mate the secrets of your power: for example, men, tell your wives how your need for her seduction became a subconscious suggestion to her to obligate her into becoming a slave of your selfish need and how your anger punished her for not being a "true" wife. That way you release her from her ancient obligation.

A woman does not mind having sex with a man who truly loves her. There is no dead end here. There is light at the end of the tunnel. No American objects to obeying a good president, but a bad president produces a revolutionary spirit in the good citizens and makes bureaucrats out of the bad ones.

Remember—foolish, wicked men obtain ego reinforcement through female love and acceptance, and that means sexual support. Don't be that kind of woman. To have sex with a wrong man is to lend support to everything that is wrong in him and to everything which he is going to do wrong to you and to the children. You are better off without that swine. Your husband cannot wake up to realize the truth as long as you meekly and fearfully play along.

Sex is the opiate that helps a fool to "remember" he is a man and to forget he is a beast. Be aware that such a man can know no loyalty to a woman. Her only value is in use, and just so long as he can use, that long will he be loyal. When he uses her up, he will seek another whom he can use. The subject of any use inherits the power to suggest, through the victim's lust. So, as a woman, only ambition will allow you to go on being used. You want something that bad? Too "bad" for you!

CHAPTER 10

Surrender!

If you were to stand perfectly still and not actively seek ego fulfillment (from need-hate experiences), you would then feel an eerie pressure of reality building within you. And if you were to be still long enough and not run, your soul would feel a pain becoming awareness of guilt, then sorrow, and finally repentance, which would resolve in an inner surrender to God. You would then feel relief; you would feel his warmth, his love, his infilling of life flowing through your spirit.

Up to this moment, your soul has not been ready or able to accept the inner will and way. You have dreamed away reality and grown in your own, old egotistical way. You've used everything to sustain a *fantasy* of yourself as God and could not relate to anything in a natural way as a tool to bring to pass the inner reality. You didn't know it, but you surrendered yourself to the things you used and lost yourself so completely that you could not see that you were being acted *through* by "friendly," treacherous wills. You awakened feeling empty and betrayed and escaped again.

Your first reaction was resentment, and that was directed at what made you aware of the truth. Resentment is tantamount to a denial of reality. It blocks the salvation that could free you from the adversary and gives you a false feeling of being all right, in charge. You were more angry at God for making you aware of your weakness than you were at yourself for having been a fool! You see, you really have two angers.

All your anger then becomes directed toward those who have hurt and betrayed you. You used your unforgivingness, your judgment on a person, to keep from realizing the judgment upon you. But hostility (being a wrong way of feeling right) only made you feel your emptiness more keenly, intensifying your ego need to be loved. And who can fulfill a need for false love but a friendly deceiver—someone you eventually come to judge and hate?

Instead of stopping to acknowledge your weakness, accepting the truth about all this, you become even angrier, because *anger* (judgment and hatred of others) *helps you focus your judgment to the exclusion of truth about yourself*. Resentment forms a chain of forgetfulness, because it focuses your attention away from the truth about yourself as the problem and upon the hate object, filling your interior world with memories nursing past injuries, to the exclusion of reality.

Certainly, you are what you think, but be aware that what your soul wants determines the *source* of your thoughts and, therefore, of what you will become. Your reality, your criterion by which all things are measured and done will appear from below or from above—from the god of fantasy and deception or from the God of truth.

As long as your sense of your own worth and greatness is paramount, you must continue to use people, places, and things to prop up your fantasy beliefs. While you believe that you are acting in your own self-interest, you will use everyone and everything in a destructive and self-destructive manner. And that, my friend, is a prelude to hating!

The consequence of the original fall (through man's use of woman) is still with us. You can see it in the intensifying of your emotional sensitivity—first in your relationships with members of the opposite sex, who champion selfishness and never self-denial, whence it spreads into every area of your life. In the stubbornness of pride, your soul turns from the true salvation of the inner light of truth, ever reaching away from, and out toward, people and things.

Man's basic, driving need for ego reinforcement ripples out to woman, pressuring her to respond ego-supportively. She must become as the dream woman of his selfish fantasies. Playing this accommodating role, she finds fulfillments of a kind in the man's failing. In the light of reality, you see such love is productive of nothing but failure. This is realization that the puffed-up male ego cannot stand, so he blames the woman for his *own* weakness. Having used her once to help him forget truth through her love, he uses her a second time to deny responsibility for a wasted life through hate and blame.

Man may indeed escape his awareness of truth through his use of woman, but then there comes a time when he must escape awareness of her dominance by the use of other pleasures—only to become betrayed and dominated on lower levels.

In surrendering to a man's need-pressure, woman, too, experiences a fall. Her own ego animal awakens through sexual identification with the man, just as the man's ego animal has awakened through her. Through woman, man becomes a woman-using creature, and through man, woman becomes a man-using creature. Their separation from God occurs through mutual abuse, which progresses to become an abominable, intolerable cycle of hate begetting love (surrender) and love begetting hate—their souls feeding like parasites on their mutual decay. Man becomes addicted to the pressure presence, the anxiety-relieving distraction of the female love-hate tease, and woman, to the pressure presence of man's sexual need. Once addicted to male pressure, if it isn't there, a woman will seduce a man for it and then turn around and hate him for being out of control!

It's quite a mystery. While it seems that they surrender to one another, the man, actually, tends to surrender more than the woman.

What I am trying to say is that we are forever *creating* pressures in order to submit to them, because for better or worse, the spirit of pressure gives us a delusion of power and of salvation at the moment of surrender—depending on whether you are the man or the woman.

Male pressure draws up something in a woman that feeds on a man as it anesthetizes his soul, growing only to the degree that his need grows, and commands hell to exist in her to serve his ego. It was man's selfishness that caused this hell to come into existence originally and incarnate itself within woman. And his selfishness remains the sole cause of our suffering.

Woman feels conflict for being man's strength; she knows she is the reason for his existence. If she doesn't like that arrangement, what can she do? *Men won't look at a woman unless she is willing to help them betray their own reality*; women actually *become* the power that men want to believe they are.

At a point in her descent, woman must also seek salvation from the pain of conflict, as must man. Her sin has been to play the goddess of love. By indulging the worst in man with her love, she has made him an animal re-created in the image of the hell in her. It is a terrible power to be able to tempt men to surrender to love, but *man demands to be tempted.* He unwittingly makes her his god, and woman's own failing, her feeling of power, begins to thrive on meeting this demand. From this chaos of loving and being loved grow conflict and guilt. From guilt comes hate, blame, and escape into judgment.

From man's demand for female complicity in his wrong, woman's hatred of man is born: and since it is just as much a sin to hate and judge the males as it is for the man to blame the woman, woman also feels guilt welling up in her for her part in the intrigue; but she is immediately tempted to compensate for her failing by an atonement of love! And now she is unwittingly supporting the problem in the man—love is her dilemma. The male's sexual response cannot pardon her sin of hate; instead, sex love feeds the ego monster in her. Thus, between the two ego-sustaining, truth-denying emotions (love and hate), the female ego puffs up like a giant cobra.

We have a love-hate relationship with everything we surrender to and care about. Anything that is loved, apart from God, becomes a source of frustration, because in surrendering, it cannot provide the fulfillment sought by the lover. Like women, to the degree that they are *used*, all earthly possessions possess. What surrenders to us is

125

what we really surrender to, substituting for a relationship man ought to have with God. Therefore, deny your selfishness. You have your chance every thoughtful moment. Seek to surrender to Him for the infilling of his approval, which is the only source of true peace and fulfillment.

As long as we reach for earthly creature comforts, we draw up the original spirit that is in agreement with our ego's secret rebellion against reality. That is the reason you are frustrated and cannot find peace. Every escape is only a deeper sleep—a fool's paradise. The point is that if we don't surrender to God for his love, in our perverted hunger for approval we will unconsciously succumb to devils for *their* love, and they will eat out our substance.

Conscience, then, is the ultimate pressure presence. It is love, knocking at the portal of our souls, waiting to come in and drive out the other, false spirit of need and love. If you could recognize that inner pressure you feel (without pressure) for what it really is, you might then experience true Salvation. Conscience is *not* your enemy, it is your true friend. See this and be careful not to create countering *external* pressures for yourself anymore. Recognize that, having been corrupted through yielding to external pressures, your inward nature has been transformed to need the spirit of external pressure. Now in you, it cries out for more of the same to grow on. It will try to trip you up in your quest for truly harmonious relationships, because it needs the old all-too-familiar love-hate pressures to continue existing through you.

There are many types of pressures that can keep you from meditating and coming to God. Anything you use for release—for example, that strategic drink—supplants your need for the true answer. You can't meditate when you are excited or upset about anything or are indulging in forbidden delights. The meditator seeks to preserve the tranquil, calm, even state of mind. His joy and life are in knowing and doing what is right. But the fool doesn't want to know what is right, since in that case, he couldn't do what makes him feel great! He *needs* excitement to motivate him, to urge him toward what his conscience would otherwise forbid, to help him forget past shame.

You simply must realize the truth about those blocks to Salvation and ask yourself what you *really* want out of life. What is your heart's *chief* desire? You may claim to want to find truth, but that could easily be foxhole religion—*any port in a storm*. You may be hurting so bad that you will try *anything*—and that just isn't good enough.

Your motive shows in all your choices. You choose now to smoke and drink, because in the past you chose some secret sin from the guilt of which you also need distraction. If you choose to feed your ego, meditation becomes impossible, because stillness would take you *toward* the reality you hate, whereas drink or love or anger takes you away from reality to the food your prideful soul wants, delivering you to the god of false love and fulfillment, before which you must debase yourself.

Physically, we all need that of which we are made. The elements of water, sunlight, and air—we must have such essentials to survive. And we all have deeper needs also, whether base or noble, that draw elements from which our characters are fashioned. When the true self is corrupted, so are all the attendant needs, which will attract us to sustenance for the altered self. Once our original

127

natures (longings) are supplanted, our hearts' yearnings are perverted to incline us toward what originally degraded us from spirit to flesh.

Be warned, therefore! Do not mistake carnal craving, and the obsessive yearning for human affection, for true Love. By locating in another the source of the "good" you need, you continue to unconsciously surrender to the god of deception that lurks behind all forms of ego pleasure. If such love-need is not recognized for what it is and *gradually transcended*, it will bring you to death's door. What is that love you seek? Surely, from the cradle to the grave, it is a selfish fascination with evil.

Realizing this, can you still tread the old path? Can you see that life is a surrender to a good—or an evil—spirit? And now that you know this, to what will you surrender? To the internal pressure of your conscience, the reality that all along has been trying to humiliate you into repentance? Or will you surrender to the intrigue of love-hate and sensual delights? *Be still and know that conscience is the divine pressure. Yield now for saving grace!* Think, before you reach for your familiar fancies.

Denial of reality is your basic problem. Keeping alive the pressure-centered image of yourself by using objects, people, and places is part of that denial process. How stubbornly selfish you are can be measured by how far you will go to gratify your ego. All your energy could go to denying truth—into trying to prove to yourself that you are *not* wrong, *not* a failure, until you will be unable to relate to anything or anyone correctly, and truth will be beyond your grasp.

On the other hand, your cravings and selfishness may be little more than inherent weaknesses that you can recognize and transcend on a day-to-day basis. This is what the maturing process is all about. Perhaps you were programed to be prideful. The hatred (resentment) so many children have for their parents habituates them to pressure, causing them to need it (a wicked parent substitute) when they grow up. All failing people need the very pressure that made them fail—in order to *become something*—to succeed. This is why a man will marry a nag like his mother, and a woman will bring out the father she hated in the man she thinks she loves.

Deep in our souls the egotist in each of us covets the position of godhead. Yet, had we been corrected from the path of egotism and selfishness, truly loved, that is, by our parents in the matter of this weakness, life would have been very different for us; but it was our parents who awakened pride in us, simply by tempting us with the wickedness of their own ignorance. Through our resentment of their rejection of God in themselves and of our truest need for Him in ourselves, a craving for evil love and acceptance sprang up. Then from each experience of such love we awoke on a lower level of hate. Hate led to love and love to hate, endlessly, till all we could feel were hate and low, painkilling pleasures—because all the love we had ever known came from *feeling and deception.*

If you were rejected by your parents, you were made to feel unworthy by virtue of the feelings of inferiority that sprang up from resentment. Your resentment of your parents set you on the path of pursuing false love, because a false persona had begun to grow up inside you (through hate!). This false identity, with its own prideful aims and intelligence, has sought completion in destructive use relationships with people, places, and things. Where there is no truth (love) in the home to stand as a correcting contrast to all that is false, there is temptation. Your resentment, being a response to that temptation, awoke in you the infant pride-god extention of your willful or weak parent, which then began to grow in conflict with your true self. To blunt the pain of this conscience, you became a selfish user.

Pride, the offspring of parental temptation in you, sees (as the parent did) the conscience as its enemy; and this drives you to seek acceptance at any cost, to sacrifice your money, your body, even your life, as the Japanese kamikaze pilots did in World War II. Having lost yourself, you seek to complete yourself in causes, in cults, in churches, in booze, in people, in sex, in drugs, and in music. Temptation operating through your father's failure to find God turned you against God and set you up to become the sensuous victim-creature of the spirit of lying love that you are. Sensual feeling love is the only love you have ever known, and through it comes more of the sickness in your soul—more conflict—and then as well, feeling (self-)punishment is the only reprimand you have ever known. That, too, is a substitute for love which only begets greater suffering.

Let's explore another way in which pride can pervert your actions. You may find yourself attracted to those your parents hate. For example, if your mother is prejudiced against black people, you may particularly gravitate to blacks. You may marry a black. Although it will appear that your choice was independently made, and you may pride yourself on your lack of prejudice and your capacity for love, your choice could easily have been dictated by a subconscious wish to get even, and not really by love for another person. In this case, you were never a friend to blacks or a black husband at all, but merely used them to support you in your resentful rebellion against your mother *and* the truth.

So the die is cast, the trap set. The variations of friends-fiends are endless. If your parents were not truly your friends, then every *friend* will turn out to be a *fiend* attracted by your selfish ego need to be served, and you pay the price of being served by becoming enslaved.

The manipulation of your soul is not the province of any single human agent, you see. Once you have become subject to manipulation from any source, its authority can be transferred throughout your entire wretched life from one person or thing to another. You may escape from your dominating mother into your supportive wife, but then your wife becomes the mother both you and your kids must now escape from! You give up overeating and surrender to smoking! Food no longer has you, but now tobacco does! Everything that serves enslaves—*except your conscience.*

Submission to the truth as we see it must be our role in both failing and virtuous states, a prerequisite to fulfillment from either a good or a wicked source. Since surrender is inevitable, why not, then, choose, now that you know where truth is, to submit to good? Regardless of our choice, we are bound to lose our identity to the greater spirit, exchanging the old for a new self that emerges through our submission. Good does not serve our egotistical aims, so we generally have little use for common sense and decent friends. But if we are willing to see things as they are, *no matter what the cost*, the truth will reveal itself to us each moment.

If now you are willing to see the truth in what I am saying about the love of the world, *you no longer will want to seek it.*

You are getting close to the truth when you find you need people and things less—that you are beginning to feel free from approval. Correcting Love wrote these words to you so you would perceive the falseness of comforting love. No longer seek acceptance, and you will not find hate or frustration. Give up hating the world—for you see that others are caught in the same trap as you—and you will have the elusive forgiveness (acceptance) and love you have been seeking. The rejection you felt as a child made you believe that God, too, had forsaken you, but that was because *resentment itself,* its nature being of wickedness, of rejecting good, cut you off from God's grace and left you craving substitutes.

Look inside yourself. Are you presently struggling against knowing the truth? Are you summoning up *hell*pmates to help you perpetuate your illusions?

And when your ego struggling has made matters worse, then what will you do? You'll get upset with yourself, of course! You continue hoping for the victorious illusion of ultimate triumph over the knowledge of your failing through *more* resentment-based *struggle.* All the while you are feeding your remaining strength to the problem, so there has to come a time when all your strength will have been consumed in the process of creating an even bigger hell. When it appears and looms bigger than you, when that awful reality makes you see the truth of what you have done, what will you do? Unable to escape from it, you will escape into it!

So, why not give up struggling now in a right way? Struggling with your problems is, after all, but another variation of denying truth. It takes energy to deny truth, and when all your energy is gone, hell, once invisible as your servant in life, will appear as your master in death, and you will surrender for the last time.

CHAPTER 11

Phony Love Is Big Business

False love is the greatest corrupter of mankind. It comforts and embraces him, even as it overwhelms his reason and robs him of his sensibilities. When you are loved in a phony way, you place your belief in that superloving being very much as you might believe in God. This love pulls you down at the very moment it is building you up with lies. From the moment you believe the lie, you cease to be your own person. You will have given power over your life to another, lower-life being. Worse, you will also have given over the authority to hypnotically suggest the terms of your existence, and you will be compelled to obey in exchange for approval.

Such mind fusion and identity confusion often begin through an unusual and undue amount of praise offering. As your ego lowers itself to accept the seductive tribute, the control of your mind and emotions is immediately transferred to the loving manipulator, whose honesty and beauty at that moment appear to be the truth you are seeking, outshining reality.

What you must beware (be aware) of at a time like this is an inherent weakness for ego food. Your unwillingness to see yourself as you are translates into a compulsive desire for approval.

If your phony friends had real love for you, they would know the danger you face from the support you want from them. They would do everything in their power to bring you back to reality. Instead, they find food for their own egos through supplying the illusions you crave, in order that their own egos might feel powerful and secure. Unfortunately, they, too, become dependent on being believed—on being a better liar. So they learn to become more conniving to keep you *falling* in love. It presents a conflict of interest for them if they really help you, because the truth would free you and threaten their parasitical existence.

It is possible to recognize the contrast between real and artificial love only if you have a deep, sincere commitment to God. Since it is by rejecting his light that we confound our senses, if instead we did *absolutely nothing* when the lie love presented itself, we would immediately differentiate between that which is real and that which is false. *Deception exists only as a result of a specific ego need to reject reality.* It may be difficult to believe that the lie you live is the result of selfishness which makes lies attractive and truth repulsive; that is why you are so easily deceived!

Truth will have his way through you if there exists the smallest yearning. Ego self-deception requires rebellion and the giving up of all our energy. The moment you are willing to stop and look, to stop feeding the illusion, the moment you hold still for a split second, the chain of command and energy transference is broken and all love-hate illusions crumble.

So it comes to pass that we can only succeed in rejecting God and his life in us by our conscious desire to become unconscious of his word. But as soon as you are willing to give up your selfish willfulness, His light instantly reverses your illusions, and your perceptions instantly begin to change. There is then a clarity of seeing that outlines all evil intentions and naturally causes you to reject the sort of love or truth which raises you in a flattering light.

The other love source assists your rebellion against the truth in your heart, and it does that by overwhelming your soul with unearned praise, flattery, and superficial kindness and generosity, as if to convince you that you are a very important being—and so, your ego becomes addicted to deception.

The temptation here is to move in the direction of glory, when just the opposite is true. The *catch* is that in order to continue feeding this illusion, you must enslave yourself to the source. You may have escaped one master (the truth) only to become entangled with another. There are no such things as freedom and being your own person. You must serve either God or the devil.

The need for recognition is the most basic and dangerous quirk of human nature. Deep down, we all have a secret delusion that we are God, if only someone would acknowledge us. This cherished hope leads us to spend our entire lives seeking our "rightful" place above other *mere mortals*. Since everyone else in the world also has this need, we run into a lot of competition, deception, and vicious rivalry along the path to mutual destruction.

Everywhere we see people playing ego games, putting one another on, putting others down in order to build themselves up, bettering themselves by their *comparison*. False love is a form of corruption and degradation which all victims revel in, because they really believe that good is happening. That is why we find ourselves surrounded by a great deal of cunning and cruelty. Phony love is very big business. You can have anything you want through it, if you are a convincing liar. You could own the world if you were *good* enough at it.

If you respond with resentment to rejection, you experience an increasing feeling of unworthiness, and this in turn makes you crave more deeply the feeling of worth that comes from a lie lover. Your own resentment actually separates you further from God, who is life. It is this truth that makes you feel unworthy, and it is this truth which is repeatedly rejected through lying love. Growing need can also make us feel people are holding out on us. When you are caught in this cycle, you literally sell your soul for a hug or comforting word. And when you are betrayed, resentment (which intensifies the need for love) is experienced.

Out of the inferiority that appears from love and hate, out of the guilt which assails you when your life energies are drained, arises the need to initiate love for others. It is possible to compensate on the surface for deep-seated feelings of unworthiness and inadequacy that others have laid on you.

The more guilt you feel, the more powerful your flowery pretense of love for others can become and here you can discover how to be the deceiver. People respond eagerly to your show of love, becoming so dependent upon it that they will do almost anything to ensure the perpetuation of false ego feelings of security. In this way, you may gain the desperately needed recognition of yourself as God, with actual (not illusory) power, simply by recognizing and cooperating with the need to be worshiped.

The only love most people have ever known is the feeling that is awakened in the presence of deception and wickedness. By making them *feel* alive and good about themselves, it can seem to you as though you have at last found the true meaning of your own existence. But you are in danger of becoming a tyrant—a monster. Your victims draw from you a lying spirit. In exchange they give you their energy, their service—their very lives.

At this point you become as dependent upon lying as your victims have become upon being lied to. If you tell the truth and otherwise hold back emotional support, the entire world you have built up on phony love collapses. Sensing the danger compels you to discover, to dredge up, new ways to cripple your helpless victim and, with cruelty and rejection, make them need and want you.

But the lover is never free from the recipient of *love*; both of you are chained together in your private hells. As each participant becomes aware of his mutual enslavement, a terrible resentment springs up and evolves between you. This resentment may serve to distract or be used to intensify any enjoyment of love; either way, you both lose sight of your failings as you sink into intrigue. The love-love, love-hate intrigue fills the emptiness of your being with a constant distraction and activity that resemble life and meaning.

When someone believes in you, it helps you to believe in yourself. It's only natural to trust those who understand your selfish ego need for love. Everyone who wishes to exist selfishly needs that special someone to help him feel special in that special way—oblivious to folly and guilt! When this foolish yearning is fertilized by contact with a phony lover, a sense of worth begins to grow, rooted in the tyranny of evil. Our friendly fiend also knows how to put you on to keep you down, to grind you into the ground for fear that your loving service will put him back in the original role of servant and, hence, victim.

So, through cruelty and violence they prevent you from loving, from seducing them from power. This is the love-hate thing that follows throughout our wretched lives. As much as our pride swells with the food of false love, so does it also manifest the extent of our sin; that is to say, the further we depart from reality, the more aware we become of our madness—but our hearts are hardened and we again and again reject the internal correction (true love) through external love.

To every egotist, the lie always seems to be genuine, while truth is viewed with suspicion as cruel and uncaring, simply because it shatters the glory he cherishes. So, it comes to pass that the egotist begins to respond to external truth just the way he does secretly to his own conscience, rejecting true friends and welcoming enemies as friends. It is a very difficult lesson to learn to be grateful for truth in all its illuminating harshness, rather than the traitorous warmth of *fiends*.

How long will it take you to see that love lies? If you could see your pathetic, unprincipled, selfish self objectively, you would see that you do not merit any respect, only contempt. Any person who can hold his nose and respect you in your unregenerate condition has to be a liar—or changed into one and then accepted for accepting you. Parents do this sort of thing to their children by expecting respect.

No wonder people take advantage and use you. No wonder you are always more depressed and hopeless. As I have said, love, while appearing to give, takes, leaving you ever more desolate, confused, and resentful. Love robbed you of the very things it promised to give! Your lover (user) has always walked away more powerful, more superior, more beautiful—and you became more drained, wretched, weak, inferior, and unworthy. Please God, you will now awaken to the awful truth that lovers are betrayers and users. If you don't presently know how to stop from being used, it is only because your ego is still committed to selfishness and the lying love that is the evil catalyst of having (and being had).

Basically, it is your own inherent weakness, carried forward from infancy, which betrays you—that part of you which desires to see itself as a great and wonderful god. Your need to be worshiped instead of doing worship (of your divine Creator) is the magnet that has summoned up the enslaving servant from out of the pit of souls. Blaming, resenting that person who does the worshiping is no answer. Remember that the guilt produced by hating makes you crave love more intensely, even the very person you hate.

The only love with which a selfish, sinful, hateful, guilty person is compatible is of the false variety, with its power to help us believe in the goodness of a *self gone wrong*. All egos are fascinated with the deceptive power of evil. Being fooled is fun. One enjoys being fooled by the magician and the seductive vocalist. You may sense you are being had, but you like the feeling. Deception captivates your attention and keeps it safe and secure from coming face-to-face with conscience. Lying and being lied to have become essential ingredients to your ego survival apart from God, as *God*.

Too much false loving can actually cause a man to feel so inferior that it can appear sometimes that his wife is too good for him. This can eventually make him resentful and impotent.

To get away from loving tyranny is difficult, because it is hard to prove the fault; so he convinces himself that he doesn't deserve her and can never measure up to the illusions she projects. And so he makes a noble excuse for his next sin of pride: out he goes to find a slut who (he thinks) is more appropriately supportive of his station, but it's happening all over again. He has forgotten that before his wife became superior to him, she was his worshiper. Remember the rule: Put someone on a pedestal and he will surely urinate on you.

Love degrades in so many mysterious ways that it invariably drives a man to violence. As soon as he gets the love he craves through violent means, he again feels more degraded than the woman he degraded, and that angers him to again inflict horrible cruelty on his partner, forcing her to service his ego *without* the pretense of love. But either way, service or servitude degrades him below the station of the woman, and it drives him wild.

Before the time of true love and grace, a woman gives a man she seduces from power just two choices: to become a wimp or to become violent to keep her from dominating him. Women tend to bring men down with love, but men generally do it with violence. Of course, the wimplike man can learn seduction from the woman, and with the roles reversed, it is the female who becomes the violent, rebellious personality.

Just as men are seduced by false love, in exactly the same fashion does bureaucratic tyranny seduce the masses. The downfall of a nation is but a variation of the horrors to be found in the home—a visible outgrowth of internal decadence.

In America the art of deceitful love is reaching the peak of its development. We are now reaping the devastation that results from deceitful, seductive bureaucratic policies. We are devolving downward through an era of personalities, entertainers, and politicians. Liberals pride themselves on their empathy for their underprivileged fellow creatures and shower them with entitlement programs such as food stamps, Social Security, Medicare, and "free" (state) education.

Little do we (or are we willing to) know the harm being perpetrated upon the so-called *underprivileged* because working society is called upon to make sacrifices to provide for the spoiling. Political love is causing our mutual destruction. The poor Americans are being used by politicians in their lust for power.

The bleeding heart is responsible for the decline of all democracies and great societies, because this sympathy is a friend of only everything that is wrong and vile in human nature. This love is an enemy of good. Remember the words of the Scripture: *The love of the world makes you an enemy of God.* Violence and depravity being the natural outgrowth of degrading love, rebellion blossoms into crime and eventually overcomes the phony system and replaces it with dictatorship and overt tyranny, with class respect going only to the most violent and ruthless.

143

Because male liberals are mostly women in men's bodies, they must operate craftily, interpreting every human need (which they cultivate in the same way as women do) as a civil right or entitlement. Like the ancient Serpent, such politicians are the ultimate embodiment of evil (sympathy), literally building palaces for welfare queens and kings on the ruins of civilization.

The impulse to liberate mankind from the consequences of his common failing is the same as that which made man fail. Politicians have adapted this theme in their quest for power, serving a need so as to become master of the greedy needy. So, you see, there definitely is a kind of love that *causes* men to fail and keeps them failing and which keeps on coming to the rescue.

Who can resist the appeals of the spoiler or degrader? False sympathy is both ego-elevating and degrading at the same time. Each high is the new spiritual low where mischief enters. The emotional high is where you are actually robbed of dignity, self-respect, self-reliance, and independence—the very things you thought you were getting. Having been separated from the *light*, there evolves in you the nature of the deceiver, which cannot stand the light of truth. Remember well the three Ds of degradation: *debility, dependence,* and *dread!*

If I were the devil, I would cultivate, encourage, coddle, and accept all the very worst qualities of so-called human nature, thereby enslaving man to me. This loathsome empathy is the most basic and diabolical of all sin offerings; indeed, it is the very core of evil. The worst sins are *not* murder, torture, homosexuality, rape, wife beating, or any other violence; they all derive from a more basic and heinous evil seed—*forbidden love*—originating through, but not limited to, the female form. False love is the matrix, the breeding ground, of all other horrors, of every imaginable hell on earth.

The greatest deception perpetrated upon the human race is the myth of woman's love. The cure it offers for ills it creates *compounds* the initial disease, simply because the cure is the cause, the very source of disease! Putting all one's faith in mere mortals (authorities), worshiping other gods before God, is the Original Sin, and how mankind revels in it! Multiply the Adam and Eve *sin*drome by two billion couples, and there you have the formula for global slavery and disaster!

Look deeply into *the principle of serving in order to ruin and rule. Love* a man's weakness until he is either a wimp or is driven to find strength in brutality. Then yield to the brutality until it becomes an irresponsible beast taking its pleasure where it can; in rape, murder, drugs, drink—all those "loves" leading inexorably to unconsciousness and finally the oblivion of death.

Phony love is the main cause of violence. It is the primary cause of big-city desolation—psychotic poverty in a land of abundance and great spiritual wealth.

Bear in mind that there is a *right* way to love, to serve, to raise up human consciousness to its potential. I have emphasized the phony side of the force to confirm what you have already suspected, so now protect yourself against it. Believe me, if you can see it for what it is, why would you want "love" anymore?

Gentlemen, do you remember noticing something odd about your wife in the first few months of marriage? Do you recall getting a glimpse of a subtle horror before it hit you? Did a strange, unspoken message flit across to you, identifying that potential evil? Did you see it like a glistening strand of spider's silk, reflecting sunlight for a brief moment before it was gone? The message was: *I've got you in my grasp now, and I am going to destroy you.*

You certainly didn't get married for love, for support. But you put her on a pedestal so that she would *worship* you in return, and because of that, you have come under a curse.

Men are fools for love. They demand *only* the dishonest kind and don't let their women be true friends. That scares them, for *honesty and purity neutralize the will to power*. Dishonest love is sexually arousing—a drug to the conscience—anesthetic to the soul. This love is such a perfect deception because it agrees perfectly with all that is wrong with us. That is why it is very difficult to see *love* as the true source of our misery. Few suspect love; *she* is the enemy within our midst. The world sings her praises, we glorify her in poetry, oblivious to the fact that we are honoring *evil*.

If a man loves a woman more than God—which is to say, he puts his own selfish feelings for her before what is wise and sensible—then he is done for. It is only a matter of time.

A man must bring a woman back to reason. He must never allow himself to be confused by her. It is one or the other; either she surrenders to his enlightened reason, or he surrenders to her confusing love and *logic*. It's a woman's lot to stress a man's soul to the limit, seeing that flash point where a man either gives in or stands firm and tall on principle.

Woman provides the "bad" stress for man to awaken and grow or to die. And man provides the positive stress for a woman to reject, and thus to die, or to yield, and thus to live. It is God's plan—his perfect justice; for if the woman submits to a man's good stress, she becomes corrected—saved from the heritage of sin—and both live unto God.

But if man submits to her spirit and accepts her love, both will die. You may now choose.

CHAPTER 12   Inside Mr. Nice

A woman has to be more careful than a man about choosing a mate. Especially, she should watch out for *Mr. Nice*, the superobliging Cheshire cat. No matter how honest and hardworking or how devoted a husband to her such a man might be, if she learns he is not devoted first to justice, to an unmistakable divine fire within, she will eat him alive. A woman deeply desires to respect her husband—so much so, that the frustration of living with a sweet but characterless animal can bring out the witch in her and drive her to drink and to other men. Unfortunately, most women are drawn to weak men—to a *Mr. Meek and Mild, the Friendly Fiend.*

Let's delve into the mystery of this weak and passive woman's man.

Good, in its purest sense, is what every woman, like it or not, needs. Fairness and firmness are the only authorities to guile. By patiently jousting with her spirit, the husband possessed of such authority can rescue his wife from the agony of pride. But agreeable Mr. Nice, by virtue of his guileful support (a sort of false love), serves instead only to frustrate and corrupt her.

149

Perhaps you see the same kind of *invisible genie* forces corrupting your children, acting through their supportive friends. You may see the danger of such friendships, but your children cannot; it is natural for their budding egos to enjoy being stroked. Their thinking is *What can be so bad about what makes me feel good?*

No mind involved in pleasure can be possessed of objectivity or foresight. It's up to you to do something to protect your children. But by standing *angrily* between them and their various craven needs (wants), you make matters worse. Your emotional interference reverses your intent, energizing their determination in favor of foolish endeavors and associations; yet if you stand silent, your seeming consent supports their faults in another way. Both that which you do and fail to do will make matters worse—and this principle holds true for just about any human situation imaginable.

Likelier than not, if you have a problem, its cause was a milquetoast or violent father. A weak dad sets one up to choose (if you are a woman) or to become (if a man) a weak husband. Being a weak man means that you have a lot more of your mother in you than you perhaps care to see, and it is her nature in you which is attracted to the same kind of female spirit (dominant-supportive) in a wife. Conversely, female offspring of a dominant mother and passive father are attracted to men they can mold and rule (or save)—for exactly the same ego reasons the mother had in marrying a weak man.

As you read on, bear in mind a theme that will recur throughout this text: dominant and supportive women are one and the same, and weak and violent men are one and the same. These apparent opposites attract and evolve evil between them.

In other words, if a man who hates his vile mother thinks to escape her by marrying a sweet, supportive woman, he has it all wrong. Submissive people pleasers are seeking the opportunity to dominate. Conquest through submission is a sneaky strategy of the weak, and marriages that begin with female submission end with female dominance. One morning the deluded male is rudely awakened to the presence in his bed of either a vicious tyrant or a hypocritical, "sweet," subtle manipulator.

The woman, for her part, chooses a man who excites her because he is malleable clay. Just as every spoiled brat loves those who let him have his way, a woman who was unloved (uncorrected) by a father will attract and favor weak men.

But she will never be comfortable with the control she thus acquires. Certainly, she may get everything she wants—all the material things—but never what she needs and *truly* wants, correction from having been spoiled. She has chosen a hopeless, romantic female worshiper who, in exchange for her approval, lets her make all the decisions and gives her everything she demands, because approval is all he lives for. In addition (another benefit), he is able to judge her for everything that goes wrong. The game of pride is to win.

Mr. Nice is never wrong in his own eyes. If he lets you be the boss, it's only because he is a born loser anyway. Too gutless to win respect by asserting himself, he gives in to you to get support for his failing and to convert failing into virtue. When things go wrong, he gets another ego boost by sitting on his perch, puffed up with pride, smiling in delirious judgment.

Every Mr. Nice is really a submissive woman inside, the wretched product of an unmanly (or absent) father and an uncorrected mother. This kind of man uses female ways to retrieve the command of his lost manhood. What typically emerges, of course, is a more submissive woman in a man's body. How can he become a real man using sly, seductive methods, surrendering in order to take charge? Will he not either strengthen his wife's role of powerful tyrant or, at best, become that power, become a tyrant himself?

In the realm of the ego, being right is equal in value to being powerful; so even though Mr. Nice's violent wife may remain as she is—a mean, masculine, animal power in the home—Mr. Nice can see himself as hard-done-by; he is *Mr. Right* by comparison with her and is thus her equal or superior. We see here the reverse of a common male-female relationship: the woman's efforts to seduce the man out of his (beastly) power succeed only in feeding his violence; but she has her consolation in seeing herself as the martyred *Mrs. Right.*

When the authority of grace is lost, a lower compensatory form of authority can appear, the authority of a jungle hell. Here again we see the classic symptom of submission at work, its desperate effort to subdue the violence that originally it caused. The cowering, frightened (guileful) female, finding she cannot make the beast she has aroused serve her cause, makes use of its evolving wickedness by comparing it with her goodness. You know the type—she is like a weak president who sees himself as a peacemaker but in fact is only appeasing and supporting evil, thus encouraging greater evil to appear, as war.

The smug hypocrisy of this type of woman promotes the evil that she needs to see in a man in order to feel the security of being superior to it. A selfish ego that cannot win power through seduction must settle for the satisfaction of judgment—the sense of self-righteousness which the slave of a vicious master enjoys. For many, the only way to glory is through the role of a tortured, brutalized slave. If a woman's ego cannot use a man one way, it will use him in another. Believe me when I say *weakness is the handmaiden of wickedness.*

Are you a frustrated, angry woman living with seductive Mr. Right? Then you know what it is like to live in a man's shoes, which hopefully will awaken in you a modicum of compassion for your poor victim. That through our sins we change roles may be God's way of helping us understand the sufferings of others. Judgment of, and seething contempt for, your parents can infect you with your parents' nature. Watch out for evidence of this in your conduct with your children.

To have a man cater to her every whim makes a woman feel so good that it can be convenient for her to believe she is in love with this Mr. Nice. Perhaps you used an available Mr. Nice to escape from an intolerable home life. If so, you have plenty of company. Perhaps you lost yourself in a Mr. Nice to escape the guilt and inferiority you felt because of hatred for a *Mr. Violent*—your father. Oh, yes, deep down you may really have wanted a good man, but you were so fearful of being dominated (even by a good man) that you were overwhelmed and taken in by Mr. Meek and Mild.

While you were cowering before your mean father and hating him, you were becoming like him inside. This is something that is hard to face, but you will see it revealed in a relationship with anyone weaker than yourself—with a weak husband or your children.

When a chance to dominate presents itself, we feel alive and powerful, important, brave, and secure. Given someone weaker to dominate, we feel relief—the same relief our parents felt in ruling us after a lifetime of being ruled themselves. Alas, these "good" feelings of security are at the expense of others; our happiness rests on the destruction of theirs, on degrading them and making them sacrifice and suffer.

It is all a deception based on the ego principle of comparison and relativity. From a basic madness, a greater madness is always evolving and manifesting. The enemy you hate and fear and would flee is inside you, becoming you!

Alas, the truly guileful are rarely awakened by suffering as the sincere person is. I am trying to say that if you can accept these hard truths, the chances are that you have been but a victim of the cycle (evil evolving evil) and, therefore, may hope for Salvation; for what child could emerge unscathed from the traumas of family violence?

What a dilemma! You run from *Mr. Mean* to Mr. Nice; then to escape the hell of power raised in you through living with a weakling, you run screaming from Mr. Nice to Mr. Mean, only to find yourself living as a weakling with the *father* you hated as a child!

Female guile is everywhere, perverting all relationships. A woman with a man inside her can be sexually attracted to a man with a woman inside him. Her maleness can make her feel as though she is married to her own mother—or to his (his mother being similar to her own).

What I am saying is that the confusing female spirit, intruding where it does not belong, fouls up all healthy life and love relationships.

When we pull away the disguise, we see Mr. Nice revealed as a female spirit occupying a male body. So long as you intoxicate yourself with the image Mr. Nice projects, you will not be aware of the exchange between you that is taking place. It can be an incredibly cunning devil, indeed. The rule of thumb is: Submission induces violence when it fails of its object, which is to ascend to power to become violent itself.

No one can escape the spirit of guile that has stalked the earth since man's fall from grace. Violent men attract submissive women—women who are conditioned to the role of mothering and spoiling violent men. And submissive men attract violent women. Everywhere there is intrigue. Nowhere is the spirit of grace to be found.

Were a businessman firm and fair with his employees, there would be no need for a union. But because he is otherwise, a union evolves, and because of its resemblance to the corrupt management, it eventually destroys the company. In the same way, graceless politics evolve suspicion, rivalry, and violence between countries. There can be no peace until there is grace.

So it is in all human affairs. When grace prevails, evil ceases to evolve, and there are no losers, only winners.

Now a generation of vipers has emerged—womanly men and manly women—seeking from each other their lost roles and powers. Like his weak father before him, who gave his wife power, Mr. Nice feels most secure (powerful or right) in the presence of a strong, dominating woman. To him weakness is not surrender, but a strategy of the ego for survival and conquest, learned from his role-exchanged parents. He may see himself as magnificently loyal, loving, benevolent, and worthy, when actually he is a cat patiently waiting for the master to leave so he can pounce on the leavings of his dinner.

Poor woman—no wonder you are confused! You cannot understand your craving for the kind of man who inspires in you only judgment and contempt. The bully who has contempt for the coward needs the coward to feel secure, because bullying is all he knows. But what does that contempt do? Does it awaken the Cowardly Lion? No, it only frightens him into a more contemptible cowardice, making the bully meaner.

When grace fails in a man, in that void left where grace no longer is, an evil (which could not otherwise be) manifests in the form of Mr. Mean and masquerades as a Mr. Nice. No matter how these two behave, they turn the wheel of chaos and confusion, of the slave-tyrant relationships that established on this planet the rule of evil and the Fall.

Can you see why Mr. Nice is no damn good and why what you have thought of as good—your good, his good, anyone's good—is nothing but a selfish game of pride? *Nice* is not necessarily the opposite of *mean;* your false good introduces and reinforces meanness, and meanness reinforces phony goodness. Such goodness is just another form of wickedness; it is the weakness that we have called *the handmaiden of evil.*

So, if you are one of those Mr.-Meek-and-Mild weaklings, expect to have a wild, frustrated wife. And if you are scratching your wooden head, wondering what it is she wants from your animal carcass, ask yourself while you are about it just why you are so nice. Are you not pleasing her in order to get her devil to grant you a sense of worth, to help you deny to yourself what you are—a fallen, miserable, selfish, wretched creep?

Certainly, you crave love from her, but only because you yourself have withheld—preferring to use her—the true love you might have given her. What she thinks of you has been more important to you than standing up for what is right, and the little good you have left in you, you are willing to sacrifice for that Brownie point of her approval. Like the first man, Adam, you don't correct your wife, because your ego *needs* the hell in her, to serve you, to reinforce your pride and ambition, to make you feel like a man, when you are not.

Your misguided mother had little tolerance for your dad's natural authority. With the power he gave up to her, her impatient, hungry spirit saw to it that male children knuckled under, thus implanting in them a nature that could survive only in relationships with dominating females.

Now you—a corrupted, womanizing man—have little concern for what is right. You enjoy being violated—and violating—with seduction and violence. Gladly and pridefully you sacrifice true worth for *feelings* of worth that women give you. You carefully cultivate and preserve a sick relationship by never offending the lady, all the while, in fact, doing her mortal harm with your loveless giving in and walking around on eggshells. (Politically speaking, liberals are like this. They are like guileful women, seeking power by cultivating the worst in society for the sake of gaining power.)

You can give a woman the true love she needs only by giving up the ego feelings of worth that you crave from her reassurances. She may have become afraid to reassure you by serving your wants, because of what this does to you both. She cannot stand for you to touch her, because of what that touch draws up in her and in you. She has seen you become a weakling or a beast and herself become a coward or beast until—if she has any honesty left—all she can do is strike out at you like a cornered animal or scream out her contempt (hopefully, with a cry to God to save her from such judgment of you), which scares you into buying her flowers!

You have become an animal, and as such, you need affection for the beast you have become. You need to be stroked like a Cheshire cat, to be comforted by your master-corrupter. You womanize and people-please for such comfort, and the gratifying of your ever-growing need to be stroked you confuse with love and goodness.

From time immemorial, a woman's body has been used (idolized) in Satanic rituals as a means of calling up the devil. Is it any wonder, sir, that your life is a living hell? What you need is grace, the kind of inward wholesomeness that does not need the reassurances of others' love and approval. Do you see how your selfish need and weakness make you part of the system? Without grace you cannot separate from it; you must evolve like an animal and submit to the animal.

Let me address myself to a Mr. Nice who has divorced and remarried, determined to try harder this time to make the marriage work. Stop for a moment and consider the pressure you feel not to repeat past mistakes, to bend over backward to please by being more kind and condescending than ever. See how your pride is still involved, struggling to make up for failure with one woman through more failure with another, instead of asking God for Salvation through his grace. You have not yet learned your lesson.

Sensing your desperation to make things work, your new (and, more often than not, sicker) wife takes every liberty she can, twisting you around her little finger, making your life doubly hellish. Because trying to make things work is the effort of will, it can be frustrated by other wills; whereas if you had no will but the Heavenly Father's, you could not be frustrated. You see, his will is there when yours is not. It is as simple as that.

You need a gracious but don't-give-a-damn-what-she-thinks-of-me outlook. Your new wife and family are expendable, in the sense that your problem can only work out if you *stop caring too much what they think of you.* You must stop trying to force this marriage to *work* (selfishly for you). You need not make up for past failings with others. The pride of life blinds and distorts facts; it can cause you to misinterpret the meaning of guilt and to think your past mistakes were caused by your not being *good enough.* Pride will not let you see your false goodness (people pleasing) as weakness, so instead of realizing and finding grace, you become *nicer* than ever.

You need humility to experience true love. You need to *love,* to care for, rather than to *be* loved and cared for; and *through patience possess ye your soul.*

A real Mr. Right is not out to win a popularity contest, nor is he so egotistical as to think he can make up for anything. Admitting wrong and not seeking support wins the approval of the Father. Therefore, there is no need to care a tinker's cuss what anyone thinks, as long as you know your course is just. With such an attitude you will be able to perceive reality, to determine what is fair and unfair. You will not concede to pressure, no matter the loss or gain. This is the manliness that evokes the respect of the real woman. Suddenly grace appears and disgrace disappears.

There are two forces working inside you. One loves the truth—and the other does not, because the truth threatens its needs. Selfishness may claim to love the truth, for appearances' sake may agree with it or even go so far as to preach it; but in practice it never gives up the fun and adventure of the egotistical life. And that is why intrigue flourishes.

For standing on principle, you may well lose the ego support of friends' approval or even sexual privileges with your wife. Suffer such rejection, and in trembling, receive grace. Fearful of losing worldly benefits, no Mr. Nice can come shining through, simply because a selfish beast is all there is of him. His entire existence depends on cultivating the wrong in the woman in order to use it.

Therefore, recognize that your need is not true love. Neutralize that need for acceptance, and be not troubled or resentful in the face of rejection. Only the real man can successfully undergo this trial. If you will, be that man; and in time, to your astonishment, you will discover you have gained your family's love and respect—because that quality appearing in you through your trial is what every woman and child is really seeking in husband and father. Once grace exists within you, evil cannot.

The vanity of a female seeks to possess what it cannot. She wants, loves, admires, and respects the man she can never have—if you see what I mean. If you give in to her subtle pressures and she gets to you, she cannot then feel respect for you, and a woman *needs* to respect her husband. Unfulfilled in this need, insecure with you, and discontented, all that remains for her is the revenge of getting to you, making you suffer in payment for your failure to be a true husband—one who would stay her with love.

Men and women are free to do good only to the degree that they are free from the need for approval. Through caring too much, you tempt your children to take advantage of your good nature and are, therefore, powerless to stop them from going astray.

Caring too much means caring only for yourself. Such caring is not caring at all, except for Number One. The man who really cares for his family, who is concerned for them, is less emotionally involved with them, so that he may stand firm on all principle—patiently—come what may. No one really respects the weak and the selfish. They are admired only to be used. Dare you speak up or stand as a correction to anyone whose favor you selfishly need? Of course not! All selfish people are bound to lose their freedom of speech and eventually all their freedoms.

More often than not we have an ulterior motive for being nice; our object is to manipulate, whether to get the mechanic to fix our car properly or to get someone to give us a job—whatever. But people aren't always fooled. The more sophisticated see through such flattery to the weakness behind it, which tempts them to take the advantage *you* are seeking from them.

When I said your family is expendable, it was to help you realize that Salvation does not depend upon your bringing anyone around. In any situation, simply hold fast patiently—through all the kicking, cursing, pressuring, and fussing—to what is clearly wise, fair, sensible, and just.

The salvation of your children and family depends on two things: 1) your standing firm on principle, making principle unmistakably clear and 2) their choosing to stand with you on the side of principle, it having been made clear to them. The choice must be theirs alone, for God wants volunteers, not conscripts; that is why you must get your own will in the matter out of the way.

Remember that your family is composed of moral beings with moral choices. You rob them of their chance to *choose* right when, in your own desperation, you pressure, manipulate, oblige, or in some way try to force them to be right. By such means you make them either rebel against you or capitulate to you in meek surrender. What point is there in sweet-talking or forcing them into being good? If you do this, it is certainly not because you care for them; rather, it is because you think by saving them, you save yourself or because your ego cannot bear another failure or because you simply enjoy power. Such an attitude will fail any marriage.

Your family can see when your concern for them to be right is not for their sake, but for its reflection on you. It is desperation on your own account that changes you from a Mr. Nice into a Mr. Mean, trying to knock some sense into your family. I'm not saying that force should not be used at times—to keep your kids from going with bad company, for instance; but it must be a force in which they recognize love, a true, fatherly caring for them.

Do you see now what I mean by *expendable*? If, through pure intent, you reveal what true caring for them is, and your family responds favorably, their choosing right is good for them and naturally pleasing to you. But if they reject the persistent good you show them, too bad for them!

They will have had their chance at life through you and you will have had your second chance. Their choosing wrong *should not faze you one little bit.* It has become their problem, not yours. You can rest assured that you did what was right. Do you see why it is not up to you to save anyone, why you are responsible only for showing the way? Your role is to stand as a contrast, not a temptation.

You cannot know how God is working to fulfill his purpose for you. He may have given you a second family to teach you a lesson and to work out a happy ending for all.

On the other hand, you may find your second family more incorrigible than the first. You may show wisdom and strength you did not have with your first family, yet still not get the response you egotistically want. That this family cannot appreciate your goodness may be another test for you. Your wife may have a wicked harlot's heart. Knowing how egotistically desperate you are, she is pleased to complicate your reaching your goal every which way she can, all the way to hell—and dragging you with her. So, there must be no will, no goal. There must be only patience and long-suffering, and never mind the outcome.

Understanding the truth, you may bring joy to a potentially good family or frustration to a wicked one. Either way, walk tall, feel gladness, smile.

CHAPTER 13

SomeKnight in ShiningArmor!

My husband recently left, and now I have the main responsibility for bringing up our little five-year-old girl.

Roy Masters: Do you resent it?

Well, I probably do.

What do you mean, you "probably do"! Of course you do. Always answer honestly yes or no—no probablies. That way I can relate to you more perfectly.

OK, then, I do.

Then you ought not. That's your problem, right there. If you resent your daughter, your daughter will grow up resenting you, feeling inadequate and guilty. You are going to project all kinds of problems into her.

I know, but we seemed to be doing such a good job together—and then he left.

Whatever the reason he left—I won't go into that now; I can guess—but whatever he did wrong or failed to do right, it shouldn't make you a bitter person. Remember, adversity can make you a better person but if it makes you a bitter person, then expect trouble with her, because she's going to feel your bitterness. She's going to feel unloved and rejected.

165

I know. That's exactly what I don't want to happen.

She's going to feel that there's something wrong with her, when in fact the wrong lies within you.

Right. One of the problems is, I don't know whether to stay here, near her father, where he can see her from time to time or . . .

Have you contact with him?

Oh, yes.

What does he say?

He thought it would be just fine to visit her, that he'd have pleasant—

What reason did he give for leaving?

He was unhappy and fed up with me.

Why? I thought you said you had something good going between you.

I thought we were bringing up the child well.

Yet, you had unhappiness between you?

Yes.

What was the nature of this unhappiness?

Well, I suppose, like most people, we just married for the wrong reason. I had a lot of resentment toward him, because he didn't give me the things in the marriage that I'd expected.

Such as—?

Such as a love life, plans for the future.

"Love life"—what does that mean to you?

Sex.

Sex? He didn't give you much sex?

No, he didn't.

Are you a very insecure lady?

Yes.

And then you probably demanded sex because you connected that with what you thought was love. You

166

not only emasculated him, but you resented him for denying you love also.

Right. But I didn't make any demands, and when I started listening to you, I began to give up my resentment. I could feel what I'd done wrong.

Ah, but you did make demands. The evidence of it is in the resentment you felt toward him for holding back.

Well, I did resent him silently. I suppose he felt it.

Yes; so you do admit resenting him?

Yes.

And do you see that it was your own resentment, backfiring, that drove him away, which made you feel even more insecure? Naturally, any man can feel a woman's resentment as a subtle demand to give up his life in place of the love he does not understand and cannot give. Your husband was suffering from the same lack of understanding, because he didn't know what it was you really wanted and never had it to give you in the first place.

Your insecurity, then, became an unreasonable pressure for love that could not be met—manifested not so much in the bad things you did, but perhaps in the too good things you did, willfully trying to obligate him for that unattainable fulfillment. We have all experienced that feeling of obligation.

Yes, well, he used to cook, and then he did his laundry as well. He didn't want me to do anything for him.

Aha! Yes—because he'd rather do things for himself than let you cater to him and feel obligated. When you see that happening, it's time to look at yourself.

I always thought that whatever was going on, we would stand together and work it out somehow, because—

167

It's still possible.

Because of our daughter.

But if you could explain, if you could tell him Look, I understand now what I did wrong. I was a typical woman indulging your weakness for love, serving you to get all your attention as if I were a god, all the while unaware that I was selfishly using, destroying you.

I know, Roy, but the thing is, he just gave up completely. He found someone else.

He did?

Yes.

Well, he will only find the same problem there with the other woman, but let's get back to you. Let's look at your resentments. They were surely there before your husband left. And you also carried resentment in your heart toward your child before your husband left.

Do you think so?

It had to be. No way can you hate your husband and love your child. Even if you thought you loved your child, it could only have been a false love, a love coming out of guilt. I have said before that resentment translates into a phony, flattering love which pulls on others to get their approval. The guilty crave that sort of love.

Right. I'm sure that's what I'm after from her.

That's exactly right. And when she doesn't conform to the pressure of this love, which you were unable to get from your husband, you resent her for that too.

She does conform at the moment, but I know she won't always, and then I'll really be destroyed.

All right, you see it, so you must take care not to do the same thing, to convert your daughter's existence in order to serve that sick love need of yours, like you did with your husband.

I can't understand where it came from.

It can come from personal ego selfishness, basically, but more often than not from your mother, whose need-hate attitude toward men, you may have absorbed.

I wanted my husband to love me so much, so I loved him like a god.

Isn't that the classic error? I'm sure you have heard me speak about that. You put his ego on a pedestal, and in that role, you became the god maker, greater than the god—dependent on deceiving—living out of his dependence on your lying love! Do you understand what I'm saying to you?

I think I do understand.

If you make your husband feel he is the boss, then you are really the boss maker, the greater boss. So, how does the man feel? Eventually, he begins to sense the betrayal, the parasite lie lurking in your supportive love. When you love a man in this way, conditioning him to need you, worshiping him (so as to be worshiped yourself), he feels the pressure, the pain, of being seduced out of his authority as a man in his own castle; he feels you living through him—his very life becoming an extension of your will.

Didn't I love him at all?

Never! Not in the slightest. You see, you have never been completely honest—you haven't admitted that it was his weakness which attracted you, that everything you did for him was a roundabout way of being good to yourself, to dominate for something women feel as security. Had you made such an admission, you would not be bitter or in this mess.

So, how do you love somebody? People do love people, don't they?

Like yourself, most people do not know what love is—and rare is the woman who has ever been loved properly by a real man. That's what's wrong with the world.

But I didn't love him only for what I thought I might get from him. I like him as a person.

No; whatever you liked as a person was slowly eroded by the way you lie-loved him. Do you see that? For instance, if you are a little bit of a thief, you may not be all that bad. There may be some good left in you, but if I keep loving you for the thief that you are, pretty soon the thief side of you would evolve, so you would become more of a thief, less and less likable as a person. In other words, the person I once liked in you would slowly dissolve into the complete thief—right?

That is the way most women love most men; their false love makes men need them. And so, in the end, even though he may be Superman in the beginning, soon there's nothing left to like, only a baby crying out for reassurance to its momma. At this point, a woman can have only contempt for what is left of the man. She may even despise her own power, and yet she will go on loving just the same, because what she has become cannot live without destroying a man.

Ideally speaking, a man should love God more than woman. But a woman is jealous of a man's introspections, his distance from her, his allegiance to some invisible order of goodness and reason within him. The guileful woman hates that relationship men have with the spirit of enlightened reason. She wants to be his god and will work hard at destroying that relationship, as a means of subjecting the man to her ego will and purpose.

But just as soon as she succeeds, she begins to feel both secure and insecure at the same time—secure because his failing serves her ego, insecure because she has become dependent on his failing, making him fail for more security. She becomes guilty of the sin of seduction. It is her nature that springs up inside the man, a nature which depends on worshiping and conceding to a woman's demands in order to have the reassurance for existing. He becomes addicted to her loving deception, as she does to his weakness, his need for that.

The man, then, is made over in the woman's likeness, craving her approval, craving that feeling of completion which comes from always yielding to her willful pressure in exchange for being loved in a false way. He becomes a woman's man. He ceases to be a godly being. Here they share a relationship similar to the proper one which might exist between man and God; that is to say, the fallen man's existence depends upon serving her wishes. It is very destructive to a man's soul to accept the treacherous love of a woman.

I know. I've heard you say this so often. But now tell me whether I should stay near this man, where he can see our daughter or whether I should go to my family in England.

I would say stay right where you are for a while. Things might change if you change. Your husband and you have a psychic bond between you. Believe it or not, he will sense this change even if you are living a hundred miles away. You could be on the other side of the earth, and he could still sense the change in you—at least he would feel a release, the way one might feel after the death of a tyrant. So release him and wait!

Do you think that's all that's wrong with me, that I look for love? And if I could just give that up—

Yes. You cannot be selfish and love at the same time. You are selfishly looking for approval for your own sick ego, turning the head of a victim toward you and away from his own spirit. To succeed in this kind of manipulation is to fail. That is what falling in love, for both man and woman, is all about. You never, never want to take a person's devotion away from the spirit of truth, the commonsense reason within him, to have that attention glorifyingly focused upon your demands in your seeking security through power.

That's a very dangerous psychological-spiritual maneuver—and were you to be successful in your confusing tactics, such attention fixed on your having your own way would drive you mad with power; you would be driven to tear men to pieces in order to feed that evolving, selfish need of yours or to punish him for failing to stop you with love. You would punish him for being weak.

I know. It debilitated me completely. I can't do anything in the house or make any simple decision. I guess I was like a black widow spider, living off my husband, and now he isn't around anymore—

Right! So, now you must look at where this insecurity comes from—from your childhood—some resentment toward your father, perhaps?

I've tried to look at how I might have had resentment for my father, and I can't really find any, except that my mother wasn't happy with him.

There it is! You see, you have taken on the identity of your mother, her sin of judgment against your father's weakness.

172

Yes, I never knew my father very well. He was kind of the strong, silent type.

And he remained sort of private, never sharing.

You're right. There was no talking or going to him for advice or anything. He was just *there.*

So, you never really knew him inside; there was no atmosphere of truth as love. In other words, he failed to save you from your mother's influence, because he himself was her victim. Can you see that because of his failing, you still have a need for a man's love? And because you have been denied it, you also share your mother's contempt for men? I'll bet that you married a man similar to your father.

Oh, yes—physically and in every other way!

Now you know what your mother felt toward your father because you are your mother, and your husband is your father. Deep down inside you, there is this need for love, true love, which he has never been able to give. His failing has bred resentment, causing you to need a love of a different sort and to unconsciously re-create your home life. You tempt a man for love, to be a real person; but when he fails you, you become a bull, and now you tempt to feed the beast you are becoming, to keep the bull alive by goring the bullfighter.

My mother developed a disease, in the end, that killed her.

I bet you fear having the same disease because you are your mother—but look at the disease you have right now; this mad, hungry ego need of yours, this ego monster that came in through your mother, manipulating to fill the emptiness of your soul. The more frustrated you

173

are, the more guilty you become and greater, then, is your need for sensuous approval by way of the failing of a man.

But the harder you try to get that approval from your husband, the more private he becomes, shutting off his emotions as a means of self-defense. You see, what you need is someone just like your father to love you in a right way. And, yet, here is this man, your husband, using you, not able to stop you from playing the ego game with the love you need. A woman needs a man who understands a woman's dilemma and who loves what is right more than his own selfish ego use of a woman; she needs a man who knows how to correct with love, how not to give in to the lie of her love and to the pressures of her hate.

But I could never figure out what he *did* want from me.

The lying love is what he wanted from you. You see, your need for love only excited the failing ego part of him to answer that need with the substance of his mind and soul. What men fail to understand is that the kind of signal a woman exudes, the teasing, seductive body language, should not be misinterpreted by men as desire for sex; it is, rather, the testing of a man's virtue, and the one who resists has the love she needs. Unfortunately, in her own ego state, the woman is also excited by the one who fails, who is weak toward her. So, she will test all men and end up picking the weakest; for only the weakest will satisfy the transplanted female need to dominate and be the power.

I think I know what you're trying to say.

You become tangled up in each other's selfishness, don't you see? You must realize that an exchange of this kind of love can never satisfy, only frustrate; therefore, stop giving that phony love of yours, and then you will be giving love! It is a divine paradox. If you resist the temptation to love (manipulate) and, conversely, to hate, your ego madness will dissolve and give way to a true and loving self. So, stop loving in that guileful way—which is to say, stop lie-loving with the aim of getting love and power in return.

If you can just learn to observe this self-serving love of yours, you will be free. All your signals will change. He will see that you are no longer giving to get, and he will be able to see himself for the first time, because he will no longer be able to judge you to forget himself. Examine your love from every angle, dear lady, and when you see its dark promise, you will find the strength to relinquish your power.

CHAPTER 14   ## Is Your Present Beloved the Tyrant of Your Past?

You respond to the conditioning of your environment only because you came into existence predisposed to doubt. Were it not for the doubt factor, you could never be subject to trauma or obligated to all sorts of tyrants.

Although doubt is a perverted faith, it nevertheless acts as a kind of faith in its negative effects. This negative faith influences everything—your mind, body, and all your relationships. Like faith, doubt is an allegiance, a deepening involvement with a manipulating but dark source of intelligence.

No matter which religious doctrine, political party, or individual personality you might believe in, all of them have a common root in doubt. The simple fact is that faith in anyone or anything external can *never* be true faith. True faith is a mystical inward experience of knowledge, wordlessly revealed. Faith stoutly resists penetration from alien sources.

Faith knows, and it knows what it knows. It trusts, and it acts on the basis of that inner knowing, and when things work out the way they should, the person in whom faith dwells has the opportunity to understand and appreciate more fully the source of his guidance and to trust it ever more deeply again and yet again.

So it comes to pass that within our consciousness we come to know and identify our true source and experience our true being. If all men were to function thus from their noblest instincts, they could never be found in their various living hells the way they now are.

The evidence of your faith, in terms of response, is really *no response*. Your emotional reaction is evidence of the collapse of your faith system.

Do you see how the emotion of resentment gives rise to doubt, guilt, and even fear? Say, for example, out of fear you become friends with your adversary and thus gain his support. Presto! Your old doubt has transformed itself into a feeling of false confidence, masquerading as faith in yourself. In your response, you see the effect of a cause rippling out from a center, reflecting and serving the good or the bad of its origin.

The question is, Are you serving someone you hate and fear? Has their confidence in you become the confidence you should have in yourself without pleasing them? If this is so, you will be afraid to displease your friend, and you will find yourself catering to his every need.

Emotional response is a form of obedience to conditioning and suggestibility. Through the electricity of your response, you take your motivation and direction from the will and purpose of its source, compelling itself into your behavior.

A will and purpose can project through you simply by your response to it. It matters little how that response was elicited. The more violent, cruel, ruthless, and senseless, the better. The more obvious a lie-love (false accusation), the better. Only through the shock generated by another, the kind that upsets you and causes you to doubt, does a life come to live in you which is not your own. And the hardest thing in the world is to own up to that fact, once we have been invaded. We defend our new allegiance with the intensity of a fight for survival, but it is not we who do the surviving!

If there was indeed a first being, Adam, who began to live backward by responding, it must have been because he doubted God and believed Satan. Only doubt could have separated him from his Maker. Our response to demands and pressures is all the evidence we need that the doubt principle is still alive and well in us today. Our life, such as it is, arises from the ego appeal to our selfish nature, the motivation from the other spirit.

The Scripture says that sin and the entire human race came through one man, that we are born in sin and must answer to its power. Ask yourself whether your predisposition to doubt is inherent. What about the hardening of your heart under stress, the tendency to seek reassurance from others, the inability to sit still? The only reason many come to realize the truth of their slavery to the world through doubt is the suffering it causes them. Sadly, some never do realize it, not ever—not because they can not, but because they will not.

The "insight" of the fallen nature rises from animal instincts awakened by the pressures of doubt. The self that is thus awakened by doubt becomes addicted to doubt. Emotionality and overreacting support this doubt. The doubt that made you a wrong person causes you to doubt again. This time you will doubt that you are wrong, and you will develop a false, temporal sense of worth and confidence. You sense that doubt is a sin, and that makes you afraid to doubt, so that you never want to doubt yourself again.

The trouble at this point is that in believing in your*self*, you are believing in an alien self, the one that doubt created. Your newfound confidence only reinforces the fallen condition. It is the same as doubting the truth again. This is why psyching yourself up, believing in yourself, being accepted and loved by others, all lead to guilt and anxiety. It is the wrong kind of confidence, you see, as it was engendered by the original fall from faith into doubt.

Good feelings are nothing but the spirit of the lie at work. Emotion seduces you into doubting the truth, strengthening the dark side of yourself. Strong emotional feelings are strangely reassuring to the dark self, the only self we will ever know once doubt has overcome faith and thus separated us from our conscience. Doubt creates emotion that connects you to the source of your sin nature; and emotion thus connected makes you doubt the truth and gives you a false faith. The result is most apparent when the feeling you are experiencing comes as what you think of as love.

Can you see how resentment can alter your inner self to need or love the hate object? And can you see how need fulfilled from that wicked source might feel like love, like completing a missing part of yourself, when actually it is completing itself in you?

After you have been very upset, notice how you crave reassuring affection, and observe also how that leads you into relations with all the wrong kinds of people. Wrong people can be very supportive indeed. In them we can find the false security we need after we have been corrupted.

The main culprit here is the resentment that caused us to be upset in the first place. The sin of resentment separates us from our most noble powers, so that now with our faith shaken, we are unable to stand firm in patience and in love to hold a mirror to the adversary's shame. As a result, we feel that it is our adversary, not God, whom we have failed.

In a sense, of course, we do hurt others when we respond to their temptation with resentment and judgment, for in so doing, we not only fail to extend love, but we add to their personal dilemma. But beware of trying to make up for that wrong. If the tempter is desirous of possessing you, he will let you try and try and try.

Your subconscious motive here is to change the wickedness of the tyrant with your love, as if you had the power of good, which you don't. This kind of love, which rises from hate as a compensation for our failure to love, energizes the wickedness of your adversary and makes him want to hurt you more. And even if he does break down and "love" you by giving you the pat on the head that you long for, all he is giving you is the reassuring lie. You become addicted to this lie, for without the shoring up of your false confidence, you begin to feel the terror and uncertainty of your original doubt.

You can never please "beloved" villains. Your attempts only anger them as they feel you manipulating their love. Very often, their displeasure or rejection is a calculated reaction designed to upset you into more boot-licking servitude. Your children, especially, feel uncomfortable with your bowing and scraping; they resent your solicitations. The reassurance you crave draws up the hell in them, but you don't know what you are doing to them.

181

They brush you aside, reject you, with meanness; and in that very moment appears the tyrant your wimpish love has brought up out of hell in order to serve you.

Servitude, you see, is the only form of goodness you have ever known, and it takes ever lower forms of evil to motivate you to show off that loving image of yourself. Do you see what you have done? You have redefined weakness and faithlessness as love and loyalty; but only a tyrant will buy your act and allow you to go on believing that you are good, noble, and brave.

A man's inherent need for approval causes him to dredge up the dominating spirit of his mother in the woman he elects to replace her. *Such a man can not or will not correct the woman's inherent wrong, because of his own insecurity, his ego need for her wrong to support his own wrong ego existence.* A love always helps you to doubt there is anything wrong with you—but you really *are* worse off for accepting love, for it means you are using that love to reject the truth. You sure are a chip off Adam's block!

Remember that the friends who have turned out to be fiends were handpicked by you, however unconsciously, for their unholy spirit of consolation. After they betray you, you become upset, and your resentment makes you want to serve them again for their approval. When a defense goes up, you are afraid to face what you have become. The truth makes you feel bad, but the lie is comforting and makes you feel good. And feeling is doubting, which leads right back to guilt and insecurity.

The rule is: Once you doubt yourself and become a slave of sin, you then tend to doubt that you are wrong in your sin state, with a little help from your *"fiends."* Hasn't that been your problem? *Fiends* and lovers have always given you false confidence in a false self; but such confidence always breaks down in the light, because it is a denial of God and of truth. And God cannot be denied forever, lest we sin unto death. Ours is, in fact, the sin of doubt, the same one that has come down to us from Adam.

Start believing. Stop resenting. Stop resenting and start believing. For heaven's sake, stop seeking love. To the degree that you admit you are wrong and to the degree that you become aware and absolutely sure you *are* wrong when you really are and don't doubt it, to that degree will you be absolutely sure when you are in the right. Just remember that right begins with repentance, and with right response comes freedom.

YOU ARE BORN WRONG. Don't ever doubt that. It will do you no good to go out into the world seeking security and approval to offset the insecurity of your sin state. Out you will go from the frying pan into the fire. Each savior who claims you will be worse than the one before.

Now let's talk about how this principle is used by the political operative, the psychopolitician, to enslave a nation. You need to see how it is being used currently to enslave the American people. The manipulator's goal is to first demoralize and dehumanize the masses, to strip them of the only threat standing in their way, virtue. Virtue is the courage the tyrant fears.

Communism cannot conquer a virtuous people, because moral people simply cannot respond, and *because* they fail to respond, they are cut off from evil suggestion and cannot translate evil's purpose on earth as it is in hell. But the beastly man is the devil's pawn, his instrument, doing his will and purpose.

Behold almost the entire world in misery, in bondage to some form of tyranny. Right here, in what was once a free nation, behold—people enslaving themselves to sex, phony religious personalities, drugs, and alcohol! Behold again—wives, husbands, battered children, all cowering in terror—every man becoming his own dictator in his own little hell.

CHAPTER 15

The Confusing Woman and the Confounded Man

According to the degree of his selfishness, a man draws to himself an appropriate mate who is both his punishment and his salvation. If he refuses to learn, she plays a part in his damnation; but if the torment in his soul awakens him, she becomes the instrument of his salvation.

The relationship between a man and a woman will be shallow—based on romantic deceptions—or deep, depending upon what they want out of it. If all they want is to use each other to glorify selfish needs and cravings, their relationship will be shallow; but true marriage is a deep experience between partners willing to set aside childish wants.

What good is a relationship if we cannot help one another grow, if we put stumbling blocks in one another's way, if we block communication for selfish motives? What's the point of talking if we never talk on a meaningful level about questions of right and wrong, of principle?

When you complain that you can't communicate, what are you really saying? Do you honestly care about other people? When you point out some fault, do you sincerely mean to be helpful and take the time to explain where you think the person is going wrong? Do you *want* to be understood, or is your purpose to confuse others (in the guise of straightening them out) about what they may see in you? Who is blocking whom?

In every relationship you will have one of the following combinations:

1) two hopelessly selfish swine.
2) two selfish people who would be otherwise if they knew how.
3) one hopelessly selfish swine and one selfish person who would be otherwise if he knew how.

Let's rule out two hopelessly selfish swine, because there is absolutely no chance of communicating with them. I say leave them alone to let them eat each other alive. I am writing to be heard by those in the second category, whose selfishness comes from ignorance, who are emotionally entangled simply because they don't know any better way.

In the third instance where there is one sensible, seeking person and one hopelessly selfish swine, the seeker must learn a calm objectivity to survive the mad accusations, ravings, and distorting of facts. He must see through the pretense of caring that is used to confuse him, and needless to say, he must steadfastly protect the children.

A sick relationship begins with a male's fascination with a female who *understands* his *needs*. To cut a long story short, he awakens one morning after the night before and finds, to his horror, not the submissive, caring, loving woman he thought he had married, but just the opposite—a pushy, demanding witch who will give him peace only if he goes along with everything she wants. She accomplishes this goal through being more and more cruel and unreasonable, frustrating all attempts to deal with her sensibly.

A man can no more correct a wife of this kind than a Nazi can correct his fuhrer, for he has elected her to support his pride, though without realizing at what price—the price of being governed by her. Whoever serves your ego enslaves it. In the pleasurable experience of being served, the governance of the soul is transferred from an inner to an outer authority, a cunning tyrant at whose caprice you suffer agony and ecstasy, trapped in an infernal dilemma of love becoming hate and hate transmuting to love until your suffering prods you to wonder *What have I done to deserve this?*

Poor ladies—the strange things you do to the men you think you love! Sometimes you just want to go up to your man and shake him, hit him, even kill him, for abdicating to you a role you can't handle. Yet, while part of you wants to waken him to save you, another part revels in your power to excite him and wants him to remain a dumb beast.

There is a kind of female whose soul is permanently bent on undermining male authority. She changes her mate into either a violent beast or a cowering, contemptible wimp who stands in silent consent to her willfulness. Her happiness lies in reversing the natural order of family life. She turns children against father to the end that they will look to her instead of to him for guidance and protection, destroying them for the sense of life and power she draws from their clinging. For the sake of simplicity, let's refer to this kind of woman as *Type A*.

Then there is a *Type B* woman, who assumes her husband's authority only through his default, because he is weak or ignorant of woman's ways and true needs. More than anything, *Type B* wants to be a real woman through the love of a real man. Her cry to a man is not for sex, but for protective caring that only a strong and righteous man can give. When she tempts a man, her unconscious purpose is to test him; is he worthy to be in charge? Is he disciplined and principled? When a man fails the test when he gives up to her his authority in exchange for sexual favors, she suffers terrible conflict.

How gladly she would yield control to a strong, caring man! But without such a man to stand up to her, the dark side of her soul is quickened. She responds with a sympathetic, seductive *love* to the loveless animal she is chained to.

Then, not meaning to, but driven by frustration, guilt, and a perverse hunger now for more and more power, she goes on to confuse and weaken her children, seductively drawing upon them to fill the emptiness of being unloved. *Type B* is a sincere woman caught in the web of Original Sin; she has inherited a power by compulsively answering her fallen mate's weak cries for help.

Far more women than men are decent inside—far more than meet the eye; there are millions of them living out their lives in hidden or open agony. But within marriage, at least, and given that she has a good husband, it is easier to be a good woman than to be a good man. To be a good husband requires being a veritable champion of virtue and wisdom.

Married to a good man, a good woman does not serve *him* so much as she does the God source within him, from which his virtue and wisdom spring. This same God source being in her, there can be little conflict; she can be a helpmate in the truest sense, working with her husband for what they both see as sensible and good. A loving, sensible woman is gifted with godly insight. She recognizes and is attracted to nobility in a man. She waits for a man with values like her own, a man she can trust to make the kinds of decisions she would make alone.

She may *serve* him, therefore, without betraying herself. That is the ideal. Having identified her champion, she simply joins her vital force to his. She feels secure, because she knows he will never take advantage of her or use her. She can be natural with him, unafraid to let her hair down and expose her weaknesses that need loving correction.

There has never been a woman born who did not have a dark side awaiting use or correction, and it is here that the concept of punishment and salvation, in the context of marriage, enters. As a rule, except she be a *Type A*, unreceptive to correction, a woman will be about as good as her husband.

In all her teasing and taunting, the decent woman is crying out for release from the serpent of power, calling to the strength in the man to keep her dark side from growing. This places an awesome responsibility upon the man. He can rescue her only if he will forego selfish use of her, and a weak and selfish man cannot resist pouring out his life to the dark side of a woman. This is because he can't stop wanting support for his ego.

He doesn't understand the ancient mystery of his need for reassurance and will be *loyal* to any old whore for the sake of sexual gratifications that briefly pacify his madness. Failing to meet his wife's real needs, a man brings upon himself a terrible vengeance, for she now allies herself with his dark side. Growing ever more willful and guileful, she will tease him for his use and use his use to dominate him.

It is not always easy to tell *Type A* from *Type B*, because all females have the same proclivity to tempt and seduce. But one with goodness in her accepts correction from a caring man with joy. For a time, she may test her powers with apparent abandon, but sooner or later she will get her fill of mischief. Her "sleeping" man need only awaken for all to be well with her—for she, too, has been merely asleep, awaiting the redeeming kiss of her Prince Charming.

But *Type A* is an incorrigible. Sensuous and predatory, she is not interested in a noble man, even though he may be dashing, handsome, and athletic. Sensing virtue, she feels threatened and is not usually attracted. Rather, she will look right past him and go for the throat of a pimply wimp or some coarse, rowdy animal with a shiny new car and money. Because of her insatiable hunger for male life, she makes a beeline for the shallow-minded, whom she can dominate and mold.

For a season a decent man may be vulnerable because of his inexperience—a *Type A* will see him as fair game and, perhaps, ensnare him. So be warned! If as one such man you feel sorry for her and try to help her, you will almost surely get sucked in.

On your way to becoming a champion, you will grow in perception, strength, and good sense, till you are able to walk away from a woman if good isn't there. But never underestimate what you may be dealing with. *Type A* is a psychic vampire, continuously scanning the horizon for sympathetic fools. She knows how to systematically "murder" a potentially decent man and his children, psychologically and emotionally.

Needless to say, there is an equally wicked *Type A* man. He is not interested in a good woman, but only in a woman who makes him feel good. And nothing will change him.

My advice to a budding champion is, don't marry too young. If you are a *Type B* man, you can control your desires; you can remain more or less aloof from the ladies, treating them respectfully, as one would a sister or a daughter. (*Type A* men cannot do this. They must use. For them there can be no relationship without use, as a woman soon finds out.)

Become reasonably accomplished in your field of endeavor—in business or some practical skill or useful profession—meanwhile gaining an understanding of woman's nature and moods through dating and friendship. If you are too impetuous, you won't have enough time to grow. If you marry too young out of need or greed, in your inexperience you will be eaten alive by *Type A or B!*

If you have already made this mistake, and the pain of matrimony has already pricked your soul to an awakening, don't panic. Don't resent your wife; after all, you married her for her tease and very likely have instructed her to be worse than she was. Pull yourself together and address yourself to the problem anew. Here is your opportunity to become a real man—not because of a woman, but despite her.

Ideally, you should wait to marry till you are mature enough to choose your mate soberly. It is best to be businesslike in all important matters; for instance, in buying a car, if you are too excited by a shiny exterior, you will be distracted from discovering troubles under the hood—then when you own the ego-building beauty, it will nickel-and-dime you to death, and you will never enjoy driving it.

I have often said to my sons, if you like a car too much, don't buy it. Let it wait, and take another look when you have cooled off. With a woman, too, if she is too *shiny*—too exciting and supportive—often there is something very wrong *under the hood*. In the same way as a car that looks better than it is, in the end she may own and drive you and nickel-and-dime you to death.

While it is true that a very exciting woman may also have a potential for good, it is not likely she will be ready to accept correction or that you will be ready to give it till you have caused each other much misery through use. Some of you will cry *Why have a woman unless she is exciting?* Precisely the point! You see, you are a user, not a lover. You surely don't want a relationship only for its excitement—or do you? Someone once said that gambling is like love: it's no fun unless you put your heart into it—but it will break you if you do.

It is man's saving grace that there is a reason for his existence. Those who feel drawn to seek this secret reason, yearning to know their role in life, are blessed. The seeker may not know he is blessed and protected, but a sincere yearning to understand life's meaning draws love—Christ's love—down from above, which separates us from sin, slavery, and death, so that nothing can harm us. There are only two yearnings. One is the yearning to understand the reason for existence, to find the uncontaminated self beyond the sewers of experience.

The selfish man's ego exists on tease, demanding seductive excitements from his mate. These excitements rule him and in time will destroy him. But a man doesn't like to hear this. He doesn't like to hear that when he is guilefully loved, he is deceived. Then he further deceives himself by transferring his guilt to the woman. From the very beginning, men have blamed women for their own downfall, which is even worse for them than the original sin itself.

Ever since Eden, the dark side of man's soul has cried out for the lying love of the mother of his fallen existence to comfort him. Just as the yearning for truth draws down life-giving love from above, selfish yearning draws a morbid love up from below.

Called to, the dark thing in woman ascends from the pit. Were it not for the female guile rising to serve the ego animal in man, the noble, true man might emerge who, with a gentle lordship, could draw the noble true woman out of his mate. Respect for a man, awakened by his caring love, seeds and develops a woman's grace and admits between husband and wife a supportiveness that cannot in any way spoil or harm.

By making herself the object of a man's love and hate, promoting in him both these emotions (one leading inexorably to the other), the guileful woman creates a subservient beast. Often, however, the *beast* rebels against the *beauty*; for just as women tease and dominate with lying love, men tease and dominate with animal violence. They oppose woman's psychic power with their physical power (or its implication).

Woman's guile changes man into beast, and the beast gets even by abusing the woman. But even though she be

193

violently abused, a woman may not be able to let go of her man. Why? Because her soul is addicted to the nectar of his life, which she draws from him through her "loving" embrace.

She feeds on the energy given off as his nature is altered through forbidden love. All men who are nurtured by tease must surrender to the role of love and hate, hate breeding guilt, which must then be "absolved" by carnal love. Their sexual love of woman represents for men the rejection of God to continue living selfishly.

The selfish man quickly loses interest in a woman he cannot arouse to a show of lying love. Conversely, a guileful woman loses interest in a man who rejects such love. Depending on her nature, a woman is either repulsed or excited by the animal in man. She knows its presence from the way a man looks at her, and if she is turned on by it, then the ancient *adventure-romance-comedy* begins, only to end in tragedy.

An inordinate sexual libido in a man reveals to the woman the insecurity of his ego. This attracts her, for she sees a need that she can feed on. Now two selfish natures take advantage and gratify themselves, receiving in a moment of ecstasy what is foolishly perceived as fulfillment—a feeling of becoming complete. In reality, in this exchange there is a degradation of the man's human qualities into those of a beast.

Degradation brings anxiety and guilt, which drive the poor beast to seek more assuaging sexual love. Do you see the problem? Sexual acceptance of the ego animal causes the soul to identify with the animal. The soothing of guilt by carnal love creates more guilt, which creates more anxiety, which creates a greater need for sexual

194

acceptance to soothe it—till man becomes a total beast, dominated by this god of malignant love. Finally there is nothing to which this animal will not stoop for a fix, and resentment of his enslaved, addicted state prevents his being restored to grace.

The compatible mate of a selfish man is a selfish woman, who seeks to become his god by accepting the worst in him.

A woman who seeks security through power over a man must be quick to prove her love through sex. Manipulative sex is scary to a woman, but her fear of it (which is, after all, nothing but sensible caution) can be thrown to the winds as a trade for power and security. Ultimately, such security is at the expense of the ruination of the man.

A woman may lower herself because she is naive and deceived—believing that sex is the way to love—or because she is worldly-wise; she knows what men want and gives it to get what she wants. Crafty, superambitious women (*Type A's*) stay ahead of the feeling of insecurity by cultivating the art of wickedness. You can see why such a woman becomes terrified when a man finds grace.

Most women find themselves obliged to trade sex for security, but a sincere woman feels miserable with her bargain and is loathe to go on playing the game. She is resentful toward her husband, because he is a bad influence, teaching her foul and whorish practices to keep him selfishly *happy*. Confused by power, she becomes afraid of his love (need) and of responding to it, for she sees that this exchange is destroying them both. She may become terrified of her husband's touch, because of the fierce, unspeakable thing it draws up from the depths of her soul. A *Type A* will be content with her bargain, however. A whore at heart, she thrives on her husband's downfall. Indeed, she feels guilty if she does *not* tease her man. She sees it as her job to keep him from being bored—to keep him too occupied, that is, with sensuality to be troubled by his guilt. Greedy for things, she feels compensated for what is required of her, by material rewards.

A *Type B* woman may be greedy for material things too; not because of selfishness (though there is always some of that), but in consequence of having been given *things* instead of love when she was a child. Deprived of what she really needed from her father, she is driven to get even with men, degrading them through sex and "demanding payment." In her frustration she demands a man's money or his life, so to speak, repeating this mistake over and over, hoping to find a man who will give her what she was always cheated out of—first by her father, then by lovers and husbands who screwed her out of love too.

In a combination of rage, vengeance, and futile searching, she gives and *gives* her body. Unable to find love, she makes do with sex, material gain, and the false feeling of security that she obtains through man's downfall. In the end, she may no longer care that in getting even with men she is destroying herself as well.

Harboring a terrible resentment, a *Type B* may meekly allow herself to be sexually abused to hold her family together. If she can manage to continue this masquerade, keeping a stiff upper lip and breathing never a word about how she really feels, her husband may go on indefinitely—fat, dumb, and happy in his marriage—unaware of his wife's hatred; but if the lid blows off and her pretense is unmasked, he awakens to find himself bonded, emotionally and psychically, to a raving witch.

If this happens, he may do one of the following:

1) awaken to face his own failing and see how his selfishness has entrapped him. Accepting blame, he will be given the grace to stop using the woman.

2) blame and hate and further degrade the woman, violently forcing from her what she no longer will meekly give.

3) run, get the hell out of there, leave her.

4) escape through the sickly sympathy of other women.

5) punish his wife by supporting wrong in the children.

6) resort to teasing and confusing, using women's weapons to get his way.

7) become a homosexual, outright.

Most men never can make the first right choice. It is not available to them, for they have never yearned to know the purpose for which they were created.

If, however, you have only lost your way for a season, I sincerely hope that reading this will bring you back to the right path.

CHAPTER 16   # The Sexxxhate Connection

The most important thing to a man is his sense of worth. Perhaps that would be all right, were it not for the fact that his sense of worth is connected to his penis.

The most important thing to a woman is security; and that would be all right too, were it not for the fact that her security usually depends on glorifying the general's genitals.

Something terrible happens when our entire lives revolve around cultivating and celebrating our sensual being. This misdirected focus of attention brings out the dark side of our natures and leads to just the opposite of what we seek—feelings of *unworthiness* and *insecuriy*.

So, then, let's explore this subject. Through understanding the dynamics of a problem, an insight may be gained into what the answer is. First it must be made clear that error cannot be conquered by force—by effort and struggle to correct it. You make your problems worse by willful effort and struggle. They can only be resolved through an evolving insight. Once you understand this, you will discover that underneath emotional upset and the expression of error are the natural worth and security you have been striving for.

Secondly you need to recognize the two sides of your nature: the natural (sensual) and the spiritual. You need to see that failure to deal with stress (in a spiritual way) is always evidenced by an evolution of the dark, sensual nature. It takes only one good belt of upset to change you and your circumstances for the worse.

This writer must assume you have read his other writings on this subject. Readers who are unfamiliar with them must take a leap in consciousness and accept for the moment the concept that spiritual failing is somehow connected to uncontrollable sex feelings—especially in men. Man's ego makes him unwilling or unable to face the truth of his failings, so he turns truth around and makes virtues of them, especially of sexual failing.

Now, you well may ask, what is failing? Failing is simply the ego struggle, the willful determination of man to become more than he was created to be. Let's take an everyday temptation for example; a person berates you and makes you feel like a fool. Immediately you become upset and start feeling inferior, so unconsciously you try to overcome this feeling by compensating.

You may not realize it, but this kind of thing has tricked you into a lifetime of frustration and failing, of making yourself worse by struggling to feel better. You knock others down to make yourself feel superior, or you seek love and acceptance to build yourself up. Temporarily you may feel better, but you are not better. You are not improved by knocking others down or by being loved in the wrong way.

There are countless other temptations that can lead us to the inferiority of pride—each of you has your story to tell, but the point is, every time your ego lowers itself to accept challenge or some kind of glory, there emerges not only some physical symptom of the failing but the anxiety that failing always provokes.

Each guilt has its own particular ego-physical manifestation; in men, the first on a very long list is an exaggerated sex impulse coupled with an exaggerated craving for a woman's acceptance. What needs to be recognized here is that there is something very wrong with any person who has an inordinate need for love.

Whenever something goes wrong in the soul, this *something wrong* craves to feel right but avoids facing the truth of its error. This is the nature of pride, which always rejects the truth by losing itself through "love." In so doing, it is, of course, involving itself more deeply in the source of its error, which in turn brings forth more symptoms. The wrong—whatever it is—is one problem, but the escape into sensuality is a second wrong, more grave than the first.

Now, every guilty one of us makes a choice, in dealing with our sins, to escape from awareness, which perpetuates the original rebellion against God, or to be still and allow the awareness of sin to catch up, bringing repentance and salvation from the guilt and the fault.

When escape is the foolish choice, the sensual nature, particularly the male sex drive, evolves. If you reject reality, wallowing like a pig in distractions of the flesh, you become the slave of deception and of fantasy—very strange rituals indeed. Here man and woman are locked in mortal conflict, boring ever deeper into one another's soul and flesh in a desperate effort to escape awareness of *what they are becoming through each other*.

When false and sensual love is used to escape painful reality, every escapade intensifies guilt, so that love becomes part of the problem you are trying to solve; *you are then escaping into the very thing you should be being freed of*. That is what it means to become a slave of the flesh or of anything.

One can even become addicted to sickness, if being sick attracts the attention and love the ego craves. Let us say you resent your mother for not caring for you; your resentment makes you sick, and now in your fallen condition of sickness, your mother gives you the tender, loving care you have always demanded.

So, you stay sick to hold on to her attention and love. It's not that you know how to stay sick, mind you, or that you deliberately got sick in the first place; what made you sick originally was the form of resentment which is aroused by rejection, and what keeps you sick is the craving for acceptance which your sickness gained for you. But now you resent having to stay sick to keep the love you crave, so you get sicker still (again, from resentment) and are rewarded with more sick love.

By this same process not only is the male ego made a slave by a very sexy, loving mama, but the sexy, loving mama discovers that her love, instead of making her man happy (as it is *supposed* to), makes him progressively more selfish, unreliable, and sex-crazy.

Among psychiatrists, guilt frustration is a major cause of suicide. How would you feel if, in spite of all your efforts, your patients got worse, though science and your own ego and logic told you they should be getting better? How would you feel if you could see all your patients actually using their sicknesses to make you feel sorry for them? Well, that's how a woman feels when her man does this sort of thing to her. Poor creature, she tries to make him happy with her love, but for all her efforts trying to please him, he only becomes a more wretched animal.

Some doctors, like heartless prostitutes, exploit their customers' needs and feel no guilt of frustration at all for staying ahead of the games—using the user. Understandably, a woman may grow heartless, too, when all her loving efforts fail; all that is left, she feels, is to outuse the man for whatever he is worth (the ungrateful swine).

A woman knows of only one kind of love—the kind she has been taught to believe men want. She dreams of romantically falling in love with a Prince Charming and of what the gift of her love will mean to him one day. When she discovers the awful reality, she feels angry, resentful, and betrayed. Her royal gift has turned Prince Charming into a frog, an irresponsible, sex-crazy beast who abuses her as thanks for her favors.

She finds herself in a *Catch-22* situation: If now she rejects her "patient" and cuts off the "treatment" (the life-support system of his ego existence), he flies into a rage; if she accommodates him, he will get sicker and more pathetically in need of a fix. As his ego existence is threatened, the patient tries to intimidate or terrify her into "treating" him. Afraid of losing him (her security) to another woman—or even afraid for her life—resentfully she gives in.

Now the details of our human tragedy begin to unfold.

Haven't you wondered why your wife, after making love, starts doing weird things that cause arguments and fighting, which then lead to *making up*? And what about this business of making up? It is somehow connected to liberty-taking and seems to license the woman to do weird, confusing things. It is almost as though your wife's loving were a way of getting inside you; and your anger is no defense, for it only sets you up to need more loving!

Men simply do not realize how much pressure their ego need places on women to respond with an *unnatural degree* of sexual acceptance, and how women hate them for this. And yet, a woman's resentment is the very cause of her giving in, in order to relieve the pressure. It doesn't, of course. The man just goes on making further demands. This vicious cycle, fueled by resentment, forms in the woman a habit of yielding for the momentary feeling of security that pleasing the man affords.

It is easy to despise women for their security need, and most men do; but what is sadder, most women despise themselves for it. They should not—for used as intended, it is a wise instinct, implanted in them for the well-being of their offspring. Were this instinct heeded as it should be, women would not give themselves to baby-men incapable of being strong fathers.

Too often, women choose their husbands as irresponsibly as if they didn't know where babies came from. Of course, many of them find themselves in such desperate straits, they have not the liberty to choose. A woman who was made to feel worthless by a browbeating father will accept a worthless man—a girl who must escape from horrors at home will go with the first pair of pants that walks by.

And there is the *Jewish princess* syndrome, which may be extended to include all women who are bred without skills; they must marry early and cling to what they get—and clinging love is what transforms men into unreasonable animals.

When sex is practiced out of resentment and for security, women get a strange charge as part of the bargain, a terrible sense of power, which the unscrupulous among them enjoy. Such a woman resents her husband for using her but becomes addicted to resenting him. Without resentment, you see, she cannot feel sufficient desire to put on a convincing show of enjoying the sex, of participating in the unholy union, the ritual from which her security of judgment derives. The need to feel secure through judgment is the basis of her sensuality, of yielding in the *sexual way that men feel as love*.

Resentment, which leads to yielding, turns the evolutionary wheel of lust-hate-lust that makes of her a lively, compatible bed partner. Female lust can come down to simply the pleasure of contemplating the next judgment *power trip* that follows sex, during which her secret store of contempt for the man is replenished.

Her need for judgment, then, breeds thoughts of sex, because it is through having sex that she gets to feel secure through judgment. She feels a bizarre superiority to the man, who, through sex, she makes into a contemptible beast; and she takes pleasure in degrading and reducing him to a dependent, whimpering dog.

As for the average woman, her guilt (of judgment) obliges her to put the man she resents back on his pedestal in order to get him to put her back on hers. Paradoxically, putting the man on a pedestal elevates the woman's spirit over his. Restored to his *place*, it excites him sexually, and so he promptly pressures her again, and his need and use of her for sex again serves her prideful judgment of him.

Blaming and hating him for her unhappiness makes her feel guilt. It is this guilt which awakens in her a desire for sex, because through it she's enabled to judge the man again and feel the superiority of judgment. So it is *that women can learn to love men they really hate.*

Preserving such a relationship troubles a decent woman deeply. Attempting to honor her husband as the boss, she finds that as boss maker she is in charge of creating a monster. She creates it with her love and condemns it with her judgment. Nothing has prepared her to handle such a situation. She may become afraid to touch her husband, realizing she has the power to destroy him and her children.

All this misery springs from the male ego—man's pressuring the woman to see him in a special light that excites him sexually, never lovingly. One way or another, she is suckered into glorifying his sexual apparatus—through psychological pressure, material rewards, actual physical force, or the simple contagion of lust. She acts the whore for him and feels like one, diminished and debased.

In reality's light, she perceives what he has made of her, which causes her to resent and *dethrone* her idol. She has the power to do it; she put him on the pedestal—she she can knock him off it. So, after lovemaking come judgment and punishment—those strange digs and betrayals leading to arguments and fights, leading again to making up through sex—a vicious cycle.

When a man and woman first gaze into each others' eyes and fall in love, the man's need seems to endow the woman with a romantic, creative power to make him glow like a god. It is as though her love transformed him or awakened him to knowing who he is, and for a time he may indeed transcend his customary self, inspired to try to be as noble as the woman's vision of him. This accounts for the maternal aspect of the woman's feelings for the man. She feels responsible for the well-being of her creation, and when he fails, she will exert herself to make him glow again. She feels sorry for him—may seem to forgive much—playing the mother.

But look carefully at where this is coming from. Old resentments, failings with other men—perhaps her father—can give a woman intolerable inferiority feelings that she must seek to relieve through sex; it does something for her crushed ego to take charge of a man.

Men know the art of making women feel sorry for them. The man is at fault. It is he who tempts the woman *to tempt him.* To enlist her support, he sends out signals of need, a kind of invisible programing, which she processes to come up with the sexual answers he wants. Neither can realize the harm of this in the beginning, but once there is an actual sexual connection, a damaging exchange occurs: the female (sensual) being in the woman is awakened at the expense of the man. Thus begins a woman's ego existence—a security dependent on the fall of man.

As I said, a man's sense of worth is connected to his genitals. To be sexually accepted is the most important thing in the world to him. Willingly he descends to a lower state of consciousness to receive his royal praise from a compliant woman. We call this descent for ego approval *falling in love.* And falling, it is; the lie of it awakens the sensual nature, triggering animal lust.

Now this ego-created animal creature applies pressure to the woman, whose acceptance accelerates the man's descent that began with an "innocent" meeting of eyes. They make love, and immediately he begins to feel anxiety (shame for his fallen condition), which afterward sets the stage and increases his need for the ego consolation that ends in sex.

As for the woman, her yielding to the pressure of his need should supposedly have made the man happy, so when he seems more wretched than before, her pride is hurt. She feels she has been tricked and used, and resentment, which becomes judgment, eventually makes her feel guilty. This could lead her to romantic thoughts. Even though she may resent the sex experience, she may tease him to need and pressure *her* for sex.

All this responding with hatred, yet yielding to pressure, slowly changes the woman's nature. Through supporting the animal in man, woman, too, becomes an animal. As I have described, some women revel in the emergence of the powers of their dark side, taking strength and pleasure in the infernal maternal game of dehumanizing men by mothering their weaknesses. But most women resent their own lower station of ruling hell. A sensible woman can never be satisfied with degrading herself to control a man. That form of security is not what she wants.

Generally speaking, female sexuality is not aroused in the way you have been led to believe. Without pressure from the man, a decent woman's natural desire for sex is comparatively weak—in some, practically nonexistent; and without false respect, man's desire would be less. Lust is awakened in a man by the ego appeal of any forbidden thing. Even stealing a cookie can stir a young man's sexual desire.

After any kind of fall (sin), a man craves a female companion to soothe his troubled soul; till he gets what he

208

wants from her off his mind, he can't get on with his business of living ambitiously and selfishly. If she obliges him, his growing problem becomes hers to deal with. Things go wrong, and he blames her. This blame isn't fair, and she knows it and resents him for it, and this—the pressure of resentment—is what arouses her; the pressure she feels usually drives her to make peace through sex.

In the history of the decline of man, woman was the initial instrument of his dehumanization. But an instrument does nothing in itself, it must be used. Man used woman to help transform his soul into the selfish beast of pride that it is today. As his form metamorphosed and he began to observe his altered state, the attendant guilt translated into a need to escape into supportive love—a love that is a lie—a lie which metamorphoses a beast from a man.

The thought desire for love (acceptance) quickly downgrades into a burning sexual drive; it's like thinking of food and becoming hungry. The thought of a woman is more an escape from truth than anything else.

So, a man having to think of a woman (to escape) ends up lusting after her, and the male ego animal cry of the man calls forth the female ego from the woman—both in conflict with each other and themselves. After sex and the excitement of the moment, man and woman become aware of reality again. Both are angry, guilty. The woman realizes she has been used, and the man feels the guilt of being the user, which makes him need to use again to escape and relieve his returned anxiety, and so it goes.

So, it is a sort of psychological pressure (which men themselves don't understand) that causes a foolish, self-seeking woman to feel sorry for, and fall in love with, a weak, selfish man. And it is the pride in man that makes him blame the woman rather than himself for everything which goes wrong in his life, all because he is not man enough to look at himself. Woman hates him for this, but the guilt of blaming gets turned around as *something wrong with her* for not inspiring him; so she feels sorry for him and, in her vainglory, tries to save him in the only way she knows how.

In other words, once a woman responds to the psychological pressure that man's need exerts upon her, she is obligated to go on being his savior-killer—an angel of death. Of course, woman has her own guilt to deal with for going along with all this for her own selfish reason; but knowing as she does that man was originally to blame for everything, she focuses on his guilt—endlessly judging and punishing him—and may never see her own sin.

Admitted or not, however, guilt is always a pressure point. Unconsciously *men use women's guilt* and make it soothe and serve them; and that false salvation is where the trouble lies.

As every woman who has tried it knows, sexual compliance to relieve a man's misery *doesn't work*. It never makes him permanently happy; he just grows more angry, violent, and sexually demanding. This is because *sex love* reinforces his fallen male ego condition, amplifying in him the very anxiety from which he seeks refuge in the woman.

It is a vicious cycle. He is discontented—threatened if he doesn't get sex and angry if he does. He feels, whether or not he understands it, that in conquering the woman, he is somehow being trapped. After the embrace, the deathlike anxiety of his fallen state floods back and makes him need a woman's salvation.

A woman of easy virtue is not at all troubled by the man's deterioration: curled up within her is such a hatred of men that she enjoys exploiting (killing) them even at the cost of dying herself. A decent woman, on the other hand, is troubled by a *"love"* life that she feels is destroying both her and her husband. She is angry and confused, feels trapped and helpless; or by comparing herself to him, she feels falsely virtuous.

With many women who become wives and mothers, a feeling of "divine" infallibility sets in. You may love them and agree with them but may never correct them, for they reject correction from a man who is not himself correct.

Some become disgusted with all men, resigning themselves to the hopeless fate of an ego life of sex-based judgments rather than have no life (no man) at all. They tend to set up in their daughters the same feelings—the *all-women-against-all-men* sort of thing. Father contributes by his pathetic, wimpish, or violent example, so it is easy to turn daughters hatefully against dad. These girls grow already addicted to contempt and judgment and so set themselves up to be sexually abused by men in order to despise them.

Are you the kind of woman who feels sorry for a man? Then you are setting your husband up to fail, for the fulfillment and the security of judgment, for a life of martyrdom for yourself, and for self-righteous suffering.

When all is said and done and sex love has come and gone, the only fulfillment an ego has left is judgment. You see, if you can't be sure of love, you can be sure of hate.

CHAPTER 17 Men Have Their Wills, Women Have Their Way

All my problems come from my husband! If he were dead, all my troubles would be over! So think most women as they proceed to kill their mates, either by indulging them sexually unto an early grave or by nagging them to death. Behold, gentlemen, the truth that every woman knows and every man is afraid to face.

The reason women so universally resent their husbands is that men the world over share the same basic weakness; that is, they use women to serve and excite their egos instead of caring for and correcting them with the love which comes only from the true Creator.

The highest form of love a man can have is the need to merge his soul with God. The lowest form is the need to merge himself with a woman, which he accomplishes through *pressuring her into a sexual union*. As his surrogate creator, she eventually re-creates him in her own image and likeness.

Whenever divine love fails to materialize as a caring for the person of woman, a mental need and animal lust take its place, preparing the man for an unhealthy ego-merging with a woman. As she responds to his need with

213

pity or to his pressure with guilt and fear, she is immediately plunged into a destructive cycle with the man. It is a terrible thing for a man to pressure a woman for sex, but for a woman to allow herself to be pressured is also a foolish thing. It is a fatal weakness.

Woman begins life as a warm, loving creature, ready to follow and serve a good man. However, the man she meets usually misuses her natural affection, compelling her to support something gone wrong inside him. His male ego perverts the healthy love—which is supportive of something good in him—until it becomes a dishonest love, a twisted loyalty to what continues to emerge in him as a selfish and thoughtless animal.

When a man needs a woman *in the worst way*, he rewards her support of the wrong in him with fake love (sex), manipulating her and depriving her of true (divine) love that might otherwise come through him to her. His preoccupation with his own selfish needs blocks the transmission of a caring love.

How can he, spiritually consumed as he is by the parasite of selfishness, give any of his diminishing substance to another? The cavern in his spirit leaves him with a craving to be filled by the woman with *her* essence. He cannot pause long enough in his desperate reaching for life, for "love," to consider the effect of his behavior upon the woman from whom he derives this ego life.

He calls his craving *love*, and he depends upon the perverse, supportive love of a woman too much to be willing to correct her—*to risk losing the life she seems to offer.*

There is something about any dishonest, ego-supportive love that awakens in every man the beast of lust and male pride. The terrible sexual pressure that this awakened animal imposes on the woman tempts her to become an animal compatible with the man. Guileful, mischievous love is the *only* love a man in this condition can tolerate. But a woman who converts to what men want women to be does so at her peril.

Man-become-animal, forever seeking arousal to escape awareness of his guilt, is capable of horrors. Believe it or not, even the warm affection of a puppy dog can make him burn with lust; he may beat or even violate that creature mercilessly, as though he were getting even with a woman.

What has gone wrong in a man cries out for external reassurance that it is *not* wrong. That cry awakens in the woman a spirit of perverse love which the man cultivates, commanding it to serve his misbegotten ego and to receive the beast in him, which was born from dishonest love.

A good rule of thumb is this: The more sex, the less love; the less sex, the more love may come through. The more sex, the less control a man has over his fallen nature, until he is a slave. True love emerges only to the degree that one can deny the ego need for acceptance of one's fallen state.

It requires a certain nobility to love a woman beyond one's own selfish need for her, but to love her more than the pleasure she provides is the true caring that is necessary if a man and woman hope to find happiness together.

All sinners crave acceptance, because acceptance enables them to persistently deny truth. Denial of truth is the sin that awakens Eros. One's need for the illusory security of approval can change one into a seductive woman or a sex-crazed man, as the case may be.

Since the Fall, we find this misplaced need in man—the crying of his soul to be joined to the spirit of corruption present in *woman* since the Fall instead of to God. Adam did not correct that spirit in woman then, and his descendants call upon it now.

Man's spiritual need for union with another (ideally, God) identifies with woman in his thoughts. Continuously thinking about woman as a means of completion awakens an ever-stronger sexual desire just as surely as thinking about food increases the appetite. It works like this—let us say that you become angry because of a wrong response to a temptation; as a result of your unappeased anger, you feel a void inside. Maybe you interpret this void as a need for food, and by thinking about food, you develop such an appetite that you eat more than you really need.

Upon discovering that you are *full but not satisfied,* perhaps you again become angry. Feeling an even bigger void than before, you again seize upon food as something that will fill you, and by dwelling on its pleasure, by *thinking about food* again, you stimulate your appetite. This is how it is with the sex needs of a man. He feels a void inside, having fallen from grace, and mistakenly he thinks what he needs is a woman.

Dwelling on thoughts of women leads to lust. But the sexual act fails to satisfy the lust—the void remains, more troubling than before, making him hunger again for the food of his thoughts. His sexual drive is intensified and perverted as this cycle is repeated. Only in God can man complete himself, but in man's mind the satisfaction of any craving is so identified with the form of woman that he turns only to her. Eventually this results in violence against the woman for her "failure" to fill him, as though it were her fault.

The cry of selfish ego need is actually a sort of signal that has the power to call upon the devil. Any need that does not move toward God *automatically* moves away from Him. You make a god of whatever your ego reaches for. As soon as the cry to woman is mystically uttered, the response to it is felt in her as a god-mother impulse to comfort and reassure. In the fall from God's grace that is implicit in this cry, sexuality—which we conveniently confuse with love—arises. *All women know the frustration of this substitution, and most of them hate men for it.*

A man's problem boils down to sex and his need for it. A woman's problem is how to cope with the man's problem. If she accepts the man as he is, he becomes a greedy abuser. If she rejects him, he feels unloved and goes off looking for support elsewhere. It's a very confusing, no-win situation for women.

This may come as a shock, but most women don't care for sex. They undergo a form of brainwashing to acquire a taste for it. However, if a woman is addicted to a secret judgmental hatred of men, you will find in her, also, a debased addiction to sex. This is not because she cares for sex, but because sex becomes the means of feeding her judgments—it becomes the basis of her ego strength. She derives from it a false sense of security, power, and superiority, which compensates her for the actual degradation the man subjects her to with his loveless sexual demands.

Do you see now how important it is for a young lady to choose the right kind of man for a partner? If she is attracted to a man who needs her to be his god, if she is flattered by such need, feels honored by it, and accepts him, time will reveal the truth of her predicament—that she is chained to a dying, selfish animal.

Fallen woman's insecurity makes her want to become a god through the worship of an inferior; this is at the root of her misguided dreams, her failure to realize that no man in his right mind will worship her as she desires. Seeing none of this, she attracts the wrong man and loves the wrong in him for the reward of his lust worship.

It is not nature, then, but pressure from the man, his need and burning, that awakens perverse female sexuality. Foolishly flattered by man's unholy attention, woman accepts the role he wants her to play; she accepts *him*, mothers the emerging beast in him. The female need to procreate would be minimal without pressure from the male.

There is such a thing as holy attention—not worship, but a caring awareness of the woman as a person. Women who want to be worshiped, however, can always spot the flattering, unholy kind of attention. They recognize that special look which pulls up out of them the mysterious, dark, essential spiritual substance which feeds the male ego. Men may have their wills, but women have their way.

There is a natural sexual affection men feel for women. This is not a problem. The problem I am discussing arises only when the man values what *he* wants more than he values what is just and wise. Then the support of a female helpmate becomes crucial.

His secret selfishness needs the services of an approving creature who is made to be lower than himself. The woman who meets this need becomes his spiritual basis, the god of a sexually rabid animal whose existence revolves around her. Her acceptance creates a forever-falling, dying man, a pleasure-seeking nothing who stays around as long as she lets him abuse her.

An ambitious man has a terrible need for a lying, sexual love. His animal nature is a sign of his ambition, a clue to his failing, which needs external support. To react to the sign is the woman's failing, which manifests as an unnatural, inordinate lust. She may even undergo what amounts to a sexual exchange, her nature so perverted that she burns for gratification as a man does.

Let us examine this.

When a woman tempts a man to fall for her, bringing out his animal nature, the observable change in the man's behavior is relatively subtle; but when a man tempts a woman to become an animal like him, the change in her is markedly apparent. Corrupted by male pressure, some women even burn for their own mothers. This is an extreme example, of course, but I want to use it to illustrate how a repeated yielding to pressure changes the immortal human into a mortal beast. *Sensuality is linked to death.*

A woman usually corrupts a man through seductive love, but a man corrupts a woman through the use of force, subtle or overt. One can actually see the effects of this force, or pressure, as it alters the identity of a woman at her core. I am not talking about the mystery of the original fall from grace, but about a here-and-now, down-to-earth, observable transformation.

When a man succumbs to temptation, an animal nature is awakened in him. This animal entity, energized by

219

a woman's response, now becomes a temptation to the woman. It pressures her to leave behind her innate understanding—to question her natural feminine reserve and become a sensual creature for the man's comfort.

A woman recognizes that something is wrong with all that pressure, and she resents it; but because it comes from a *physically dominating man*, she feels required to react. Reacting with resentment makes her doubt the truth in her heart, and she falls, becoming less a woman, less a human—to the degree that she becomes more a female, more an animal.

Women do not tempt men so much as *men tempt women to tempt them*! Men need to realize what a terribly cruel thing it is to manipulate women for their sympathy and then degrade them in service to their growing sexual appetite. Using her to feed the perverted beast in himself, man actually dehumanizes woman, reducing her to an animal state!

With the exception of Jesus, a man hasn't yet been born who has not used a woman's love to support his foolish pride: but if a man persists in this game, he will never find the true Salvation of his Creator.

Crying out to the source of his finite identity, a man scans the field for a compatible mate and locates her through her response to his need and pressure—*his cry*. But how is a woman initially set up to give this response? Why does a woman accept this sort of man? True, a good man is hard to find; but some are worse than others, and women flock to them.

A woman is cursed to need a substitute for the father who failed her or that she never had. If, as a child, she never felt the corrective love of a decent father (which she needed), she cannot recognize a capacity for real love in the men she considers for her own mate.

If her father was weak or cruel or violent or a molester, for his sins of omission or commission, she will hate men in general and will become ensnared in the trap of reacting to all men with resentment-based judgment. Now she is ready to pass on this legacy to her own children; she may never consciously know the origin of her problem or discover its solution.

That a woman can come to hate an overtly cruel man needs no explaining—she is clearly his victim. But a weak wimp of a man can apply pressure as effectively as a bully—it's just that his brand of cruelty is harder to spot; consequently, the woman he rules feels intolerable guilt for hating what appears as a nice (but weak) man.

A weak man pressures his wife and daughters to support him by making them feel sorry for his weakness. He is an artist of manipulation. If they fall to resenting him, he becomes even more pathetic and seemingly impotent, thereby reinforcing his claim upon their sympathy, till they end up "loving" him all the more to ease the guilt they feel for hating him.

Do you see now how hatred becomes love—which again turns to hatred? This cycle can create an addiction in the manipulated participants so that, if the object of their hatred were removed, they would seek another to take his place. They need some wimp to feel sorry for, to preserve their egos from realizing the sin of their judgment—they need *securities*.

Remember the basic brainwashing principle: pressure produces "love." You react to it with resentment at first and become upset. Once you experience resentment (hatred and judgment of the person who upset you), you need to experience it again and again to keep from feeling guilty for your first wrong reaction. You can't stop the cycle without admitting your sin, and you aren't willing to do that; so you continue till you are out of control. The built-up repressed hate becomes unbearable, and for relief, you give in to the pressure; you accept (love) its source.

Let us say that the hate object is your father, who is economically and physically your superior. If the internal pressure of your resentment is not expressed as violence, a strange phenomenon occurs. Hate metamorphoses to a warm feeling of love, of surrender, and *more often than not* is accompanied by an erotic desire for the hate object! You must, of course, repress this inadmissible aspect of what you feel, but it will surface when you meet a man like your father—you will be irresistibly drawn to him.

Always the guilt of hatred eventually becomes too painful to contain. If a person does not vent his rage through rebellion or violence, he must sublimate it by seeking the acceptance and approval of the hated person. It is as though by catering to the object of his hate (even creating one), he were *atoning* for the violence he has committed against the hate object—in his heart, if not in actuality.

This catering, or pandering, makes the hated person feel like a king, which makes him more dominating than before, which increases the other's resentment!

A corrupted woman's romantic dreams—which draw to her a love-hate mate—are, in actuality, her ego longings for a contemptible father. They represent a desire to re-create, in a husband, the father failure, from which her hate-oriented identity sprang and attaches. To this kind of woman, all men are alike. There is no love, only sex and abuse. Her only option for survival (of a sort) is to let herself be used while she outuses the user!

Do you see what a distorted sense of selfhood is here? The woman fills the emptiness of her life with failings and *things* as substitutes for love. Beyond that, with or without material compensations, her ultimate security rests on feelings of contempt for the man, her judgment of him as worse than herself. She uses his use to make herself feel superior to the beast she nourishes who nourishes the dominant hell in her.

You see, once caught in the cycle of resentment-atonement, it becomes virtually impossible to break out of it, *unless* you become willing to face the truth of what you have become and give up the ego gratification of tempting and then judging your partner.

From the woman's point of view, any cruelty inflicted on her by the man serves to justify her opinion of him and, therefore, her opinion of herself as a superior being. If he tries to straighten up and fly right, she is left with the frustration of not being able to go on judging him, which gives her something else to resent him for!

The same is true for the man; any support a woman gives him in his degenerate condition only makes him feel like king of the hill, entitled to continue to use and dominate her. Withdrawal of her support leaves him aware of his own beastliness, an awareness he then escapes in feelings of animosity toward the woman for denying him his right to use her.

It's a true test of a person's commitment to truth, of his willingness to see himself as he really is, if someone who has been judging him decides to give up doing so. He may go to great lengths to provoke the repentant one into resuming his former behavior—for no longer to be judged and resented leaves a disturbing void. The game over, no other player reacting to what he does, his conduct is exposed to his own view.

The sudden withdrawal of the ego support of another's reactions may shake us up enough to make us change or send us desperately searching for another player to share our death game.

You have learned that the ego can thrive on either love or hate, but when the truth is revealed to a woman that there is no true love in her home—that what she thought was love is only use—that awakening becomes the potential basis for secret or open revenge. Indulging in contemptuous judgment, her one consolation, the emptiness of her soul is filled with a wicked pride that distracts her from the realization of her miserable state.

The ultimate judgment is murder. Fifty percent of all murders are committed in love-barren homes. Lovelessness is more devastating to a woman than a man can comprehend, and her response of outusing his use is seen by him as insanely wicked. So, they go on hating each other into guilt and sensual love and hate again, until one may finally kill the other.

No matter how low a human being sinks, no matter how vile the manifestation of his sin—homosexuality or whatever—a sinner will always seek someone to worship him for his symptom to help him deny reality.

I have spent a lot of time describing symptoms of sin. There is a basic cause behind these conditions, however, and until you come to grips with this basic cause, your efforts to rid yourself of symptoms will be fruitless. The cause is this—your denial of your dependence upon your Creator for all things.

As long as you struggle to be your own final authority, refusing to recognize the true and only source of life—which is God—that long will you entwine yourself in intrigues and miseries, trying to fill the emptiness in your soul with external things: but your soul can be filled only by your Creator. Almost anything may seem to fill you for short periods of time, but all substitutes eventually pall, leaving a greater longing for the eternal life that you need.

In our egotism we confuse a need for God with a need for stimulation from the world. It is because we deny the truth of our relatedness to God that we resort to vainly using people and things to satisfy our spiritual hunger. In so doing, gradually but surely we change, physically and spiritually, from eternal beings to mortal, earthbound animals.

But if we will abandon our egos and admit our dependence, giving up the pursuit of happiness, of life in externals, then we will gain a perspective which will enable us to see all things in terms of their real significance, so that we can make appropriate decisions based on the direction of God's spirit within us.

CHAPTER 18

Marriage:
It Doesn't Have to
Be a Living Hell

If you put a man on one desert island and a woman on another, they will be just two creatures living out their lives. But bring them together, and their chemistry, so-called, produces not only offspring, but misery and chaos as well.

The human soul is a conduit through which a heaven or hell on earth can be transmitted and spread abroad. Which will occur, heaven or hell, depends on how a man and woman become one.

A woman's world is different from a man's. *Men and women live in different dimensions.* Therefore, for them to come together, either the man must cross the border to join his soul to the woman's in her world, or the woman must cross it and join with the man in his.

Unfortunately, very few women ever know the joy of leaving their world behind and becoming one with the man in his realm. This is because men have lost their way, their paradise. They keep joining themselves and their power to something in women, making hells for themselves and their children.

For a man or woman alone, there is no heaven, no hell. But join male to female, and all hell breaks loose, evolving on earth as it is in Hades. Reverse the order—join female to male—and behold! Paradise lost is found.

What is the difference? you well might ask. Two people getting married are two people getting married, you say. But, not so! One must look deeper to probe the mystery of happiness. Two people coming together as one flesh, ignorant of their heritage, are drawn by ancient mutual needs to be supported in their weaknesses by each other. From his fallen nature has evolved man's unnatural appetites and terrible need for woman. And out of her original failing—the meeting of that need—has evolved woman's inordinate need to be needed.

When male need and its counterpart, the female's need to be needed, join, the man's weakness evolves to the point of crippling and eventually killing him. And, just as man's need for ego consolation increases with being *satisfied* by woman, woman's need to be needed increases through her consoling and comforting of man. Being needed makes her feel useful, and so she encourages man's need. She comes to see her "usefulness" to man—helping him to exist pridefully—as the reason for her existence.

Men and women have problems because of this wrong kind of coming together. Encouraging need so as to grow in the pride of usefulness, the woman weakens the man to a point of contemptible dependency. To justify and glorify her existence, to make her happy, he is obliged to regress instead of grow—to become a little boy. If that is what has happened to your man, if he has changed, it is because you had to change him to *have* him. That is the change all women see in all their men.

Now, I ask you, how can any sensible man be happy needing a woman more and more? How can he feel good about being enslaved and debilitated? And how can any thinking, decent woman be happy to see the effect of her supportive *love*?

Have, therefore, perfect honor. Observe courtship protocol. Postpone sex till marriage, and don't rush into marriage out of need. Be of good (moral) intent. Good intentions evidenced by restraint will, in part, ensure that the woman marries the man, not the other way around. The woman must take time and be given time to perceive the true man within her suitor, to whose gentle lordship she can then subject herself in marriage, trusting in his subjugation to the spirit of his dimension.

There is a moral, metaphysical basis for the time-nonored protocols of courtship and marriage. The woman should never be seductive, must not trick a man into marriage by addicting him to her through sexual favors or obligating him by becoming pregnant. What kind of life will she have with a man she wins through underhanded means? The moment he breaks the rules and steps across from his realm to use her selfishly, he becomes guilty. By developing a weakness for her *love* before marriage, he leaves behind the divine ground of being in his own dimension, where he *and she* might have been protected from the spirit of the woman's dimension.

In woman's dimension there is a quiet, subtle, danger-ous, and malevolent force, a spirit that is only manifested when a man joins with a woman in a forbidden way. A man is not aware of this spirit unless he becomes involved with it by trespassing into woman's realm—then it begins to suck out his essence, filling itself and becoming the ruling flesh of hell, the ever-hungry, never-satisfied, need-to-be-needed monster of the id. It is with this monstrous spirit, not the woman herself, that a man joins when he leaves his dimension for hers.

Any inordinate need rouses a sleeping monster to take advantage of that need. Need excites greed and confers power. It awakens the larceny in friends and makes them fiends. Dope pushers were once ordinary people whose natures were altered by response to those in need of a fix. Anyone too eager to buy makes the seller greedy. Do you ever remember buying something you knew you couldn't afford, setting aside common sense and paying such a high price for it that you didn't enjoy it when you got it?

Consider the doper's need and his pusher. The greater the need for the drug, the more payment the pusher requires for it. The ultimate price is the addict's life itself. Purchase by purchase, he has bred his own guilt and frustration and nourished the evil of his *servant*. He is caught in an underworld system that thrives on cultivating need. The power and greed and false security of every pusher rest on the need of the buyer.

I say this because we are all addicts in one form or another. It's only a matter of time before all your relationships built on need and use must bring you to the brink of disaster. Need has to do mostly with relieving guilt in a wrong way. Drinking is a classic example: you drink to relieve guilt, which makes you more guilty, which increases your need for relief from guilt—which increases your drinking.

As I said, the pusher is only an ordinary man who has tasted power and an easy life and become corrupted, addicting himself to supplying his victim for the continued sense of power it gives him.

It is the weakness of man that tempts woman. It is his need that arouses the dormant spirit in her to serve it and taste his essence and become like the tiger which, having once tasted human flesh, is spoiled from eating anything else. Then instead of admitting and facing his weakness, foolish man blames woman for everything gone wrong, for all his frustrations—which spring, in fact, from his need (use) of her.

All problems in the home arise first from the husband's sickly need and, second, from his blaming the woman. This projection of his blame is another step down from the original weakness that generated all his troubles. Surely you know the name of that weakness. If not, let me pose a question: What is it in a man that won't let him admit fault? The answer is, of course, *pride*—ego. What else makes us choose to flout conscience, to fail (fall), and to blame?

Having once been called into service and tasted the essence of man, the actual woman dies. She dies in the sense that her natural appetite has been corrupted and she has become separated from her own vital, original ground of being. Substituted for it is the life essence of the man, on which she henceforth must feed to survive, cursed to an existence dependent on man's need of her. Woman and man are now like the pusher and the addict.

Now let us discuss the woman's ego selfishness, born of the man's.

Corrupted woman can never have the man she wants, because in tempting (teasing) him to get him, she changes him. The moment she *gets* him, he no longer is the person he was. Why? Because he has not dealt with her in a moral way; he has fallen to her guile.

To get her man, a corrupt woman locates his particular weakness and caters to it until she becomes his supply. Such *love* changes the man into a beast and the woman into a psychic vampire—a she-creature who tries to cheat death by drinking the man's essence, teasing him to death. Whatever values and character the man may have had, they disintegrate as he eagerly and selfishly enjoys the woman's debased demonstrations of "*love*." What I am saying is that woman's natural inclination to truly love is perverted by man's use, till all that remains for her with any man is to be an object of use, deriving from man's need of her the sense of life and security she needs.

In due course the "love" between addict-husband and pusher-wife biodegrades, baring their true natures. They are not a pretty sight, a deadbeat bore of a husband and a demanding nag of a wife, both bewildered, wondering what the hell happened to "*what we had together, our beautiful love.*" What happened to romance? The glorious life they planned? It was all a dream, of course—the fantasy that men prefer to reality, but a fantasy, nevertheless, which cannot be sustained *in reality*.

Through suffering, the woman awakens to reality. And, when she looks around and sees that all men are alike and that there is no love to be found in any relationship, she hardens her heart. Cynical thoughts and rationales begin to arise: *If I am going to be used,* she broods, *I may as well get something for it.* Dangerous ideas enter the minds of falling men and women. Deprived of love, a woman's usual revenge is to go after material compensations; but eventually her terrible frustration may make her demand the very life of her disappointing victim, because there is nothing left of him to feed her contempt.

The enjoyment of glory in any form—but especially as romantic acceptance—is a sentence of death. Man doesn't know, and doesn't want to know, that a glorious life is a curse and that for glorifying his sexuality, he forfeits his life. And while he dies through his sexual fantasies, his use of the woman is killing her. Indeed, as I have said, she is dead already, existing like a vampire on his essence, diminishing his life while she drinks from him. The sense of glory that a man and woman feel during the romantic phase of their relationship quickly deteriorates, and they find themselves in a jungle hell of sex and violence.

Behold, then, the mystery of a woman's *love*—if you have the stomach for the truth. It is a living hell. Why? Because man was meant to be a source of love, not a seeker of love from woman. The family should revolve around a *him*, not a *her*. Read on, and see what I mean.

Man was created to be dependent on inner light. His substance is from the elements, but his life is from the truth in his heart, as the flower's life is from the sun. He is part heaven, part earth, and just as a flower withers and dies without the warm, nurturing rays of the sun, when man is cut off from his sun, he loses his power; the character of the Son (of God) in him begins to fade.

The beauty of the flower is the contained celestial energy of the sun, and the noble worth, the goodness of any man, does not originate with him, but is from his Creator. What if it were possible for the flower to want to be the sun, to be the very light that made it? Then the flower could not be. What I am saying is that *everything must have its place to be anything.*

While the flower cannot conceive of being the sun—let alone strive toward such a goal—prideful, vainglorious man may choose to aspire to what he cannot be.

How do you go about setting yourself up as *God*? Through having someone worship you, of course. It begins in your mind—thoughts, images, fantasies. You see yourself being worshiped and dispensing judgments. You cannot *be* God unless you think others think you are and accept you as their judge.

Absorbed in fantasy, sustained by what appears to be reality—a woman playing along—man is separated from the light. He exists now as an omnipotent god, reigning from his throne of postures and achievements. Man uses everything to sustain selfish illusions of worth and make himself feel important. He is monarch of his realm, like a little kid in his playroom. Little does he suspect that the opposite of what he intends is happening. Playing with his toy soldiers, becoming more and more involved with them till he cannot see reality, he thinks he is a big general, but he is merely a fool.

Woman, too, covets glory—wants to be God. A seemingly passive, unambitious *little housewife* may live entirely in her fantasies of being worshiped. Women con their husbands, using them for their purpose, desiring to be to them what only God should be: their all-in-all.

Notice a woman's jealousy of her husband's enjoyment of a quiet, contemplative mood (or of a football game, for that matter). She is a jealous god. She wants his attention more and more, until she has it all. She wants to be the source of what he feels and thinks—wants him to need and cleave to her, as he should need and cleave only to his Creator. In her pride her ghoulish *love* blinds her to her own best interest. She cannot see that any goodness in man must come from a deep and abiding relationship with God in mystery.

What inspires woman to the perversion of her role is man's weakness, his eagerness for the forbidden way. She knows what her lying affections can do. Ever since Eve every mother—all mothers are Eves—has taken a little part of her male children and put in their place a part of herself, which is bound to come back for completeness—and does—in the form of loyalty to women instead of to God.

That, basically, is the chemistry of love at first sight: a womanizer is seeking his god, the ground of his fallen being. Woman born of man, in answering man's need of her, keeps sinking to new lows of lying and aggravation, which keeps him ever interested, discovering her instead of God. Man born of woman enjoys adventuring and will (un)naturally complete himself with a woman (making a complete ass of himself).

True life comes from being objective—separate from all that is given to us in this world for proper use. The self must be free from others and from things if it is to be bonded with truth. Our original bonding with God was broken by the Fall, when woman-oriented man appeared, with his need for woman, his originator.

Love (cleave to) God, and live—or be God through the support of woman, and die.

It is the woman's unconscious cooperation, her admiration of the man, that tempts him away from his own dimension. Growing ever more enslaved to her, he loses paradise, and hell on earth appears. He stays ahead of the Hound of Heaven by involving himself ever more deeply in sensuous escapes.

The first man was given a choice no other could have: he might be sinless. He could have chosen eternal goodness to flower in him as everlasting life. The sun, moon, and stars, the birds and flowers—all but man have their beings according to immutable laws of nature. They cannot choose, and so they cannot disobey, cannot sin, cannot love. They cannot glorify God through their wonder and awe. They cannot worship, for worship is an acknowledgment of God as God, and they have not the consciousness for that. Consciousness is a little bit of God in us that enables us to know him and to exist in awe of him.

No other creatures are free to manifest the divine character as are the children of God. Nothing can be other than it was created to be, and so it is only man who can participate in his own destiny. He can bring order into his chaotic existence without disturbing the mechanical, loveless, regimented order of the natural universe.

Out of love, God gave the first living soul His supreme gift, free will. For goodness to be, freedom to choose or reject it had to be. Man's choice between good and evil would either be his downfall or would confirm his imperishable, eternal character as God's offspring. It could be no other way. There can be no claim to virtue without temptation, no courage without danger. But God in his infinite wisdom knew man would fall and in His infinite mercy, provided a plan to save him.

To this day each man falls for the supportive love of a woman; he falls away from worshiping God to be worshiped himself. Thus the serpentine spirit of evil is spread abroad upon this darkening earth.

If the truth is in a man's heart, he can love a woman truly. Love between man and woman can be a mutual

236

recognition of the living truth in each of them—but the sin of pride debases what should be an inner relationship into an external one, worldly and sensual. Woman's supportive fleshly love now becomes the man's truth. And the more guilty a man becomes for this betrayal of God, the more lying "*truth*" he needs to glorify his lowly existence. His conscience tries to tell him what a fool he is for *love*, but the spirit of the fallen woman within and without doesn't want him to hear.

Sooner or later every man becomes pathetically or violently love-crazy, fearful of what he needs. He sees he has been trapped and degraded, stripped of independence and self-respect.

There is no way out unless he will awaken and repent. To find life and true happiness, he must lay down his ego-animal life; that is to say, he must give up seeking acceptance. For it is his desire for acceptance, fulfilled in reality or merely in his mind, that awakens his senses and sets him aflame on the course of nature, *the cycle of life and death*. Look carefully at your yearning, then, to reach out and touch someone. Realize that this compulsion is nothing more than your guilty ego reaching away from reality toward the renewing of pride.

Weak, vain people base their entire existence on what other people think. But any lowlife can make you feel special—the lower the better—if you see what I mean. The truth is that everyone who seeks to be special *isn't*; and everyone who doesn't seek to be special *is*. In the moment that you give up this desire to be something special, your sick need begins to dissolve; you step into a higher dimension of being. In that moment others will see a different man standing there, strong with authority and power. The Holy Spirit informs us to the degree that our love of what is right triumphs over selfish need.

If a man cares more for a woman than he does for principle, it is the beginning of the end. He loses his balance, his spiritual power, and in place of a man, we see a lovesick wretch who lives and dies for the woman's acceptance—his truth. Accepted or rejected by her, his state is one of misery, because the appetite for death disguised as life cannot be satisfied. The day you see clearly and repent and restore to first place in your heart what is right, that day will you experience true respect from your family and begin to establish paradise in your home.

The experts tell us it is normal to seek acceptance: but this is a lie. The need for acceptance is a symptom of sin. The hankering for worldly recognition diminishes the soul, which must stoop to win it. For God's sake, then, abandon vainglorious dreams; set aside your will; let there be light and goodness in your life.

Woman, what do you want from a man? Can you get it by seducing him or nagging him for it? Does he even have it to give you? Of course not; so back off. Look at your need to be needed as a sickness. Don't feel sorry for any man. That is a trap. Don't be impressed by worldly power or wealth—that is a trap. What have you ever gotten for answering a man's cry of need but a wimp or a violent animal?

Adam's beauty was never Adam's. It was God's nature in him, hidden yet manifest, before the Fall. But then Adam changed—became the first of an endless line of lovers clinging pathetically to their Eves. If any man would seek Redemption, let him remember it was the original sin of use that led to Adam's fall from grace; Adam listened to Eve, for her favor.

A man in his way and a woman in hers may enter the kingdom. Through suffering, a man may discover the folly of pride and come to repentance. Then, slowly but surely, the guiding light within will lead him to shrink away from fixations, uses, and attachments, to become remolded and renewed. If a woman would seek Redemption, she must observe herself giving in to pressure from men—must realize that it is not love to feel sorry for a man and help him to perdition by relieving his guilt through sex.

This is the woman's dilemma: what should she do about a man's crying? How should she respond? The answer is, not at all. *And if this means she lives her life without a man, so be it.* She must not be afraid to go it alone. Let her remember the terrible power she has, to kill by accepting wrong in a man, and wait however long she must for a man of principle.

The law of inverse proportion applies: the less the need, the more worthy the man is of a woman's true respect. A man must abandon graciously the pleasures of youth.

A word of caution: there are wrong reasons and wrong ways to stop using a woman. *It is not love* to go from use to neglect—to what amounts to abandoning her. Only a restored fidelity to God can motivate a caring change in a man. If his *heart is in the right place,* he will lose interest in other women, not in his wife. He remains a man, attracted to her, but not with the old fixation, rather with a protective concern.

CHAPTER 19

The Problems of Becoming One Flesh

The palaces of kings are built on the ruins of Paradise, said Thomas Paine, and he was right. Behind the turmoil of life—the tragic conflict between the sexes—there is a story, a script that we are all unconsciously acting out. It is a story about error, Original Sin—Adam's and Eve's—with the entire cast of characters, the human race, making the same mistakes over and over as they play out their roles. Every man makes the same mistake with woman. He cannot stop, and she cannot help going along; both are bound for the same tragic end.

The role we are all acting out was cast for us at birth. It is the same role that our parents and their parents before them played, all the way back to the beginning of the human race. If it is true that we are all making the same mistake, it must have started somewhere.

Before you laugh about the biblical story of a paradise lost, read on. You will see it's not so funny. All of us have certain symptoms, and symptoms tell a tale if you can read their meaning. If the apple trees in your orchard wither and change color, they are telling you where you failed—that you did not give them enough water or nitrogen.

241

I am asking you to explore with me the meaning of your symptoms. Learn to read what your life means in terms of failing and how that failing evolves by your repetition of Original Sin. Word by word, read for yourself how you have been programmed to fall for the same old line over and over, as it has been all through the ages and shall be even to the end of the world. Indeed, it will cause the end of the world.

The human soul is a conduit through which heaven or hell may pass, to be spread abroad upon this earth. Depending upon how two people, a man and a woman, become one, they will suffer under the curse of hell or enjoy the blessings of heaven.

Should man join with woman or woman with man? To answer this question, which we *must* ask, we must delve into the nature of the needs and loves of men and women.

Every craven need contains two basic elements: one, physical-psychological and the other, mystical. Guilt, because it is born of a prideful attitude, always transmutes into an emotional need for security, which is sought in people, places, and things. Our earthly desires are hungers that result from our being cut off from an inner life support. They evolve through the polarizing of the consciousness.

You know how a magnet repels the same pole and attracts its compatible opposite. Well, in a similar way, the soul's secret sin of pride repels the inner spiritual life and compensates for its loss with fleshly and material fulfillments. This process of compensating develops an insatiable appetite for earthly experience.

But people, places, and things cannot substitute for what has been lost. On the contrary, through greed more and more of the real self is lost; one's hunger increases. And as the soul, trying to make up from below what was lost from above, stubbornly rejects the truth, the ego animal comes to life with newer hungers.

All men compensate for their spiritual dying (evidenced by their growing need) with what they call love—from which more death is made. The compulsive love of, for, and from, the world causes the male ego to fall deeply asleep to reality, materializing a creature of a lower order of consciousness, an insecure animal ruled by cravings and dominated by woman.

By original design, man is both corporeal and spiritual. Unfortunately, once the balance of his nature is disturbed, the flesh tends to evolve *at the expense of* the spirit. The man of grace and wisdom declines. In form he may appear to be the same, but gradually through sin, every atom of his being becomes mortified, as if he were turning into petrified wood. All men resolve their problems by resenting *reality*, their spiritual side, which would show them their plight.

Lover by lover, a man spirals downward out of control—something else being in control—a fact he does not care to acknowledge. His ego answer always reinforces the ego deception that caused the original fall. Man's fall in Eden was from spirit to flesh. What we experience in our lives is something like the second fall—corporeal man becoming degenerate man.

As a man descends, at war with the truth in his soul, woman becomes his drug, the source and soother of his guilt. *It is always the same story. Guilt creates the need for acceptance, and being accepted or loved* leads to greater guilt. It is the anguish of losing his spiritual life that

243

drives man to ravage the world—people, places, and things—for a sense of life to compensate for the lost spiritual life.

Sin, then, is what makes us crave acceptance, for which we unconsciously allow ourselves to be ravaged. Trying to *get our own* back, the life essence we have lost through sin, we suck on each other like vampires. All primitive rituals involve the soul's escape into a compensating vessel—beginning with man's sacrifice of his own soul to satisfy woman's need to be needed.

To seek love is to seek glory (the promise of the Serpent in Eden). To accept that love is the same as reinforcing the original wrong of rejecting God again. Woman's spirit has displaced God's spirit in man. That is why he looks to her for his continued support. He has become of the earth. More often than not, contemporary man cries for his mother or his lover to save him as he dies.

But woman is helpless to save her creation. As it is for every animal, the life of man born of woman is a cycle. Adam rejected God by choice. Fallen man rejects Him because of an inexplicable compulsion to survive *as an animal* through a woman's love. For this ego animal to survive, man must elude painful reality, and to do this he must burrow into other flesh.

In every support relationship, there is an invisible exchange going on. Psychic energy (soul life) is always being drawn from the victim by the dominant ego, the comforter, whose hunger for power increases as he or she feeds. The victim does not at first see himself as victim; he sees himself as being served. But he is losing his identity to the servant-exploiter-comforter, being emptied of himself and filled with an alien self.

Once this exchange has begun, the victim hungers for completion of the new self, crying out to the source of his corruption for more corrupting love to complete his corrupted being. When completed, he will be a complete fool in a living hell. Vileness and wickedness and death will have been completed in him.

The principle is the same, whatever the corruption—music, drugs, or alcohol. One can be seduced by the spirit of a church or of education and need more and more churchgoing or more and more schooling. The point is that man's cry should be to the Creator of the soul, not to its corrupter.

Man must learn from his mistake through the suffering it causes.

Man is born of woman in the sense that man changes through his failing with her. Spiritual man became carnal man through his use of woman to glorify himself, thus rejecting God. Now as a dying, corporeal animal, no longer a deathless, spiritual being, man begets copies of himself, literally born of woman rather than of God—as Adam was. To this day each man's condition worsens as he seeks to allay through sex the anxiety of his fallen existence. Eve became the mother of us all, and fallen man keeps running to *momma* to be comforted through the making of baby Adams and Eves.

The Bible says clearly that through one man's sin the entire human race came into existence, and through one man, Jesus Christ, that sin may be expunged.

There is a clear connection between spiritual dying and the evolution of animal man, with his awakened procreative desire. Procreation is life born of death. The fact of death drives us to replace ourselves—to survive as animals, at least—to continue as a species. But we are not mere animals. An animal's life is fully realized in its cycle of birth, maturation, copulation, procreation, and death. But man was given more and must seek to realize it. To live but the life of the flesh mortifies his soul.

Man was created to be eternal, imperishable—but through the transgression of pride, he *died*, fell asleep to the reality in which he once existed. He awakened to find himself in a new dimension of consciousness, in new circumstances; for consciousness, after all, dictates conditions. He awakened as an animal, full of anxiety for the guilt of his fall, drawn to woman for comfort in his shame.

All men feel shame for being woman-using animals existing under a sentence of death. But what does our prideful ego force us to do? We keep on wallowing in the flesh, sinning to feel sensuously alive rather than seeing the truth that we are dying to the flesh through our sins. In ignorance we reject the truth—as Adam did. Imperishable life was his, and he forfeited it in his pride!

We are deceived by death posing as a vivacious, scintillating life form. It was *through (not because of)* woman that corruption entered man. It was not, nor is it to this day, woman who caused, or causes, man's falling. Adam's motives and desires were understood by the spirit in the Serpent, not by Eve. She was but an instrument. Through her, Satan tempted man, and in that moment Adam's spiritual eyes were closed and his physical eyes opened, and he saw Eve as never before and instantly became imprinted with her female body.

The first object a gosling sees as it emerges from the egg, it accepts as its mother and naturally follows it around for security. Even so, *man has followed woman* for his security since his first awakening as a carnal being. The spirit that used woman to corrupt man entered man through his use. Do you see the principle?

Man, as sinner, was *released* through a woman. In his pride the first man harkened to the flattering Tempter, and in that instant his soul's eye was darkened; the pure, paradisiacal life faded, and with a changed perception he beheld woman as flesh and was imprinted by that view. His spiritual authority vanished.

If the Tempter, the Dragon of Old, had incarnated into a donut instead of into Eve, Adam would have been imprinted by the donut instead of by woman. Believe it or not, he would have had overt sexual feelings, as well as submerged longings, for donuts. He would have felt that something missing could be supplied by having sex with a donut. He would have been capable of being in love with a donut and loyal to a donut.

But the Tempter knew what he was doing when he chose woman to be his instrument. Reverse the order of faith, and woman, who responds to man, will instead cause man to respond to her and to her spirit. It is *her nature to be entwined with man*. That is why man must be her guide and protector.

And, so, to this very day, as she supports her man in his selfish ego ambitions, she actually cooperates in his decline, even misconstruing it as a duty that she should do so. Of course, the more supportive she is, the more damage she does, however *loving* her intent. As she feeds man's pride through her acceptance of him, he grows more and more afraid of opening his eyes to the truth—more and more dependent upon the distraction she provides.

As long as a man feels there is any hope of acceptance by a woman, any possibility of finding that special person, that special comforter, around the next corner, he will yearn continuously for worldly love.

Shaming conscience drives man to seek refuge in the foliage of imagination and memory, where the reinforcing spirit of the lie of Eden lurks, appealingly concealed in the image of the female. He fantasizes acceptance in the form of easily available sex.

Erotic ideas that a man habitually calls to mind are not mere images, harmless indulgence. Behind the pictures he can see, stands the spirit of darkness he can't see, enticing the soul away from God's merciful Salvation toward a hideous salvation of its own. Fantasy leads to more fantasy and to an ever-increasing sensual burning fed, but never satisfied, by daydreams.

Imagining the forbidden leads to seeking out an actual experience. Thus the spirit that dwells in fantasy incarnates itself through sick fulfillments.

Original Sin began in the soul and is perpetuated in the mind—not only through stray thoughts that come to us unbidden, but *through the indulgence of such thoughts*. The soul, by escaping into fantasy, repeats in unconscious dreams Adam's rejection of God.

It is dream indulgence that awakens sexual burning, which, through experience, materializes degenerate man. Be warned: your dreams will be nightmares, and the spirit of your nightmares will, stage by stage, open your eyes to its presence on lower levels.

Sexual thoughts and feelings may arise in connection with anything, because of the soul's inclination to take comfort where it can. Anything at all that can successfully appeal to the comfort-seeking ego will arouse sexual feelings toward it. Any trauma (experienced shock) produces an identification with the agent of the trauma, whether it be a person, place, or thing.

At the moment of trauma, we open our eyes and are imprinted by what we see, which, in a sense, becomes our new ground of being and through which we seek completeness and sympathy for our plight. Thereafter we will be compulsively drawn to the traumatizing agent, tormented by a growing incompleteness that in turn becomes a sexual drive seeking union with its god. Instant gratification causes instant spiritual agony, forcing us to escape reality through fantasy and sensual pleasure centered on the corrupter.

Marooned on a desert island, sailors dream of food and sex. Perverted man will dream of donuts or German Shepherds—he will seek completion through relieving his sexual tensions with women, animals, vegetables, even pictures in girlie magazines. If you were violated in the back seat of a blue '46 Chevy, then you will fantasize being violated again by the same kind of creature in the back seat of a blue '46 Chevy.

Traumatized man is dehumanized—a robot beast—the devil's pawn. And his touch draws up the worst in woman to serve and glorify the worst evolving in him.

Remember, woman is not so much corrupted as she is *unloved*. All the blame belongs to all men since Adam. It was man who corrupted himself with woman by using her to support his ego when he should have corrected her to express the Father's divine love. Since the Fall, all women come into the world possessed of a spirit of guile, which invites either use or loving correction.

It is man's need, his prideful yearning, that seduces woman to respond with ego support; the man, failing to meet her need, is met with her, and they descend together. Her response to wrong with a wrong of her own generates in the man an increased guilt, a yearning for more wrong-supportive responses from her.

Men are so self-centered that they believe women exist only to serve their egos. A woman seeks the loving, correcting father she has never known. A man seeks the familiar, indulgent mother who changed his diapers.

Can a father correct a daughter if his self-centered purpose for marriage is nothing more than to use his wife to support his ego, to obligate her to indulge him like a spoiled brat? Surely there can be no love there for the wife or for the children that his use of her begets.

So a girl grows up with an uncaring father and unloved mother, feeling she needs something from a man and not knowing *what it is*. Along comes a pathetic creature, whose need, rippling out to her in waves, programs her to feel sorry for him. What can she do but answer in the old way, as Eve answered Adam in Paradise? She gives her "love" to make him well and happy—and behold! Out pops the beast! The knight in shining armor is transformed into a treacherous slob, a wimp, or a ravager.

We may say we *love* ice cream, for instance, but man and woman were meant to love each other in a better way than that. When a man uses a woman, she feels he is absorbing her as if she were ice cream on a plate. She feels him nurturing his selfish, wicked ego on her flesh, drawing up from within her a responding yet dominating, ugly, flesh-hungry entity. In this way, just as Eve did, woman again and again becomes the spoiling mother of

250

the emerging beast, a dominant she-spirit in the home who destroys her offspring with a ravaging love.

An unloved woman cannot truly love her children, be they male or female. Rather, she infects them with her need—her sons particularly, who grow up to seek in marriage a spoiling spirit to replace her in the form of a wife. So, from generation to generation the story is repeated, the same script indelibly inscribed on man, who by his father's default and his mother's spoiling, is unable to love a woman but uses his wife instead of correcting her and begets with her a progeny of uncorrected females and corrupted males.

There are many horrible complications and perversions in this ongoing drama. And the pity of it is, all the while we are in paradise but once removed, a garden deteriorated into a hellish jungle. The same tragedy is reenacted everywhere, through billions of different bodies, units called families making up the total insanity of nations.

Let me express the idea again. Try to view everything in this text as variations on a theme.

Once a man corrupts a woman to acknowledge him as God, he places her on a pedestal and bows down to the evil in her. This is what his love amounts to: worship of her for worshiping him. Not until he tries to stand up to her does he discover what has happened. *The ego needs evil to exist, to serve its pride.*

Man who is served by woman cannot correct her—he is not right himself, and he has become her subject. Even if he could correct her, he wouldn't, because his ego existence depends upon the evil in her, which really needs correcting. You see woman's dilemma. Through no great fault of her own, she has become man's earth god—a sacrilege for which man and woman pay with their souls.

251

Disorder is our heritage. Only through deception and disorder can the indwelling Dragon of Old continue to evolve his own order on earth as it is in hell. He knows how to get to man through woman: *Because thou hast harkened to the voice of woman . . . dust thou art and unto dust thou shalt return.*

We men are, indeed, still foolishly listening to our wives. Like spoiled kids, we still need them, because we need their permission to exist selfishly. We need their acceptance. We cannot bear rejection. We will do almost anything to keep from being rejected. Acceptance is ego survival (till it kills us).

If you, as a woman, allowed yourself to become an object of use, you must have thought there was something in it for you; and if you found yourself used, and you continued to allow it, there must have been certain rewards. You must have liked the power and the glory that being used conferred, as your user's need of you increased.

Once a woman has been used and has tasted the power, glimpsed the possibilities, a spirit of willfulness takes over, a dark intelligence that becomes her guide. It teaches her the rules of the game—how to exist through deception and the ruination of man.

Women, don't be too hard on yourselves. You are not wicked. What is wicked is a spirit that has made a home in you by way of man's use or neglect, beginning with your father, who failed you. Some of you let yourselves be used to stay ahead of the shame of your relationship with men. In continuing this practice, you feel shame, because you think what is happening to your mate is your fault, your sin.

252

Taught by men that your spoiling love is a cure-all, you do more harm by becoming more supportive, a "better" lover. Meaning to help, you let your guilty husband escape into you as you absorb him into yourself. And while you comfort him as if he were your baby, hell sucks the two of you up.

As I have said, people, places, or things can be objects of use. A person who is an object of use may be called a lover but is, in fact, one who harms through comforting and supporting. A female lover can, as I have explained, fulfill her own selfish goals by outusing the user. But she pays a terrible price, a ruined family life. Her own natural life source ceases to flow as she becomes addicted to the life essence flowing out of her mate. Even if she realizes the truth, she is helpless. She must continue to use the user, for she has no life source of her own. Her mate's death becomes her way of life.

Man begins life dominated by his mother, from whom he escapes to join himself to a wife who finishes off what mother began. If he escapes his wife, it will be with a whore. Or he may escape into drugs, drink, or music or into some malignant pseudoreligion. He will find a lover and something or someone to be his petty dictator and parasite.

All of the ruling elite in politics and entertainment are elected to be used like women, to cater to the feelings and fantasies of those who elected them. Whoever gets to be your answer gets to be your god. Depending upon the type of answer we want, each of us descends into our own particular private hell.

To the guilty ego, the *real answer* is the problem. The answer I allude to is *conscience*, of course. The more stubbornly we reject conscience as the answer, seeing it as the problem instead, the more glowingly does the false answer (and real problem) shine in the dark. We become ever fascinated with *beautiful* evil, with its power to distract us from reality.

Entertainments that exist solely to distract us do so indeed, but from the sleep they induce we awaken to be imprinted and programed by nightmares, from which we then must seek escape in a yet deeper sleep of distraction. We refuse to wake up from our dream fulfillments, yet we must sometimes; and when we do so, it is always to a darker horror of what we are becoming.

The real answer to the problem that comes from living in a dream is to awaken and stay awake. We must suffer the harsh light of conscience *and consciousness* and allow repentance to come.

Those who want to be your answer don't want to see you straighten out. They don't want you to become an aware being, because the very existence and perpetuation of their selfish kingdom depends on always being your answer. Every dyed-in-the-wool vampire wants to go on being your lover god and is hellbent on preserving its sick existence with you at the expense of your life.

Your *answer* exists to deceive you because you need and choose to be deceived—you want to glamorize your falling condition. And so, you have love-hate relationships with all manner of scoundrels who serve your stupefied soul by keeping you submerged in your dreams.

The girl of your dreams turns out to be a nightmare of schemes. By enraging you, she drives you to seek deeper refuge in her flesh and others'. How many times will you reject reality as the answer and choose instead the dreams hell is made of?

When you have a problem, how do you see it? You fail to realize how it is that you see a problem at all. If you would stop and have the good sense to ask *"What is showing me that I have a problem?"* you would know the answer must be *"My conscience."* Your conscience has been trying to tell you something all along about transgression; but you haven't been listening, or you heard its voice and thought it was the enemy, the problem.

Out of guilt you keep hiding in the foliage of your mind, as Adam tried to hide from God when he had disobeyed. *"Why do you hide from me?"* asked God. *"I was ashamed because I was naked,"* Adam said. God asked, *"Who told you you were naked?"*

No one had to tell him; Adam was self-conscious, as all of us become when we sin. There comes a day when there is nowhere left to hide from God except in the dark hole of death.

Your conscience, my friend, is not your enemy. Conscience is the original ground of your being, the spirit of your true self beckoning you home.

Every man knows in his heart that he has failed woman. He may not know where or how and may never want to know—but the nagging sense that something is wrong, which he seeks to escape, is the patient voice of his conscience, never completely silent, waiting to be heard.

Dear reader, before you saw these words, you may have had the excuse of ignorance, but now you do not. From now on, whenever you look at your problem, remember what the answer really is. *Man*, look at your need for woman in a different light. *Woman*, look at your supportive *love*.

CHAPTER 20

So What is Real Love?

Love is giving and taking, need and the fulfillment of need. If, sensing your thirst, I were to offer you a cup of cold water, my offer could be an expression of love; but if my gesture were to contain any motivation other than the simple fulfillment of your need—if I were motivated by a desire to manipulate your opinion of me, for instance, or to gain control of you in any way—there would be no love at all in my offer. And if your perception was not clouded by any hidden motivation of your own, you would sense my lovelessness. You might accept the water, of course, and thank me for it, but you wouldn't deliver yourself into my hands for it.

True love is innocent and free, no strings attached. It gives and goes merrily on its way. False love poisons and possesses. But—alas!—How many of us are so pure in heart that we have not, at some time, fallen prey to the blandishments of manipulating love? It's like drinking salt water. You drink, and your thirst increases until it becomes a craving and drives you to drink more and more, until the salt in the water kills you. If you knew where to find fresh water, you would gladly go there and drink it.

Even so, would you seek out true love if you knew where to find it? Our need for love is as basic and vital as our need for water. So many of us are drawn to the poisoned well of *love to drink deeply, desperately, compulsively*, even though we know it will kill us in the end.

Before you say to yourself *Well, my love is pure; he can't be talking about me!* please take a good look at your relationships with those around you. By his rebelliousness, your "ungrateful" son might be trying to communicate something that he cannot find words for; or the violent behavior of your husband might be saying *Stop loving me; stop possessing me. You're eating me alive!*

If he runs to the fountainhead of another's love, he is saying that your love has become too destructive, demanding, and degrading. He thinks, of course, that the other woman's love is different, but he has forgotten how it all started with you. He may find fresher water, but he will be hooked by the same old bait. After all, it worked for you—why shouldn't it work as well for her?

Do you remember what your thoughts were as you set the hook? Do you recall your secret motive? Did you not know in your heart that you could not be entirely honest with him and *expect to have him at the same time*? Did you not realize that you had to pretend to have thoughts and emotions that you did not have, that you had to exalt his ego, bring him down with flattery, and lock him in with sex? It worked of course. He soon became dependent on your false love. When he did, you felt that it was safe to start reeling in your catch—your turn to finagle some fulfillment for your own selfish needs.

But when the poor fish felt the tug on the line, he felt betrayed by the bait. He began to see your *love* in a different light and to doubt the purity of your motives. 'Twas ever thus. Love on the rebound is such a universally experienced phenomenon because we are all so hungry for love that we refuse to learn by experience. We simply get off one line to be hooked by another. Only hungry fish bite. The hungry ego never gets to be a wise old fish. So, what is real love? Well, for one thing, it does not tempt.

A recent TV ad for a chemical sweetener sells its product by saying "It isn't fattening; it isn't bad for your teeth—it's just plain satisfying"; and true love is a lot like that. You can get to be a wise old fish if you can learn to identify the bait with the hook and leave it alone. Just let it wiggle in its provocative, ego-tantalizing way, the way that turns on all the ego-hungry fools, and know that you don't need it. It has nothing to offer you once you realize that true love lies within you, trying to tell you what love is not.

As I started out to say, love, whether pure or false, is need. Need is a prerequisite to fulfillment. No need—no appetite, no fulfillment—no love. Using need as a measurement of love, it's fair to say that the greater the need, the greater the capacity to appreciate and experience love's fulfillment, the blessed kind or the other. Love from within sustains the real person. Love from without appeals to the ego and sustains the pride. It also exacts a price: life itself.

A big tree has a greater need for sunlight, its life source, than it had as a seedling. A little tree fulfills itself with small amounts of light that slowly transform it into a giant plant, a beautiful, light-dependent form. The solid mass of the plant is, in effect, *light* manifested as a living creation. The plant's cry, its hunger, is the yearning need of the created thing for its creator source. In this case, it is the light from the sun. In the highest, purest sense, need is the only love a living being is capable of knowing. Just as the tree is required to stand in the light, soaking up rays of sunshine, so ought we to walk and live in the light of our conscience.

But what if we fall from the true light? What if we are corrupted—altered by seduction to need seduction's love? We should already know the answer to that question, for we are all fallen beings, existing in a reversed state of consciousness on a diet of false love. In his carnal condition, man mistakes the offerings of a woman for the assurance he needs from his Creator. As he wallows in the *light* of woman's love, nurtured by her presence, he cuts himself off from the true light and, in his weakened condition, soon earns the contempt of the very woman to whom he has fallen.

Ancient peoples worshiped the sun, for they saw how it seemed to give life to everything. There it was, ever present, giving—never taking—life. Surely, they thought, the sun is the source of all creation. But just as the sunlight causes plants and bodies to grow, evil can become a source of false life to rebellious, selfish egos—so much so that if they were to be cut off from the evil growth factor, their ego selves would cease to exist.

It is written that the Serpent was the most subtle of all the creatures in the Garden, for it carefully avoided direct contact with the first man. It sensed that its enslaving motive would too easily have been observed and resisted by the light that shone through Adam; so it seduced Eve, planting its guile in her and altering ever so subtly the form of her love; and Adam was deceived by it. To this day, that love lurking in the uncorrected (and, therefore, unloved) form scans the horizon for Adams, seeking to find the same hairline crack in their natures which existed in Adam's—the same susceptibility to the notion that they have a right to aspire to the forbidden role of the god-head, supported by what appears to be Eve's loving agreement.

Such a man draws so much strength for his ambition to be God from the woman's deceitfulness that gradually a strange change of focus begins to take place in his nature, and he begins to see her as the center of his existence, the god that he himself has aspired to be. The uncorrected woman whom he should have brought to the light becomes the *light*, the god, of his own life. Most men love women more than they love God; they love them as God.

Evil love has no life of its own, so it must live on the life it tempts from others. The warmth men feel in the company of women is the miasma of their own decay. The love they feel is the ecstasy of their soul's dying.

Men are so egotistical that they take little notice of how their bodies are deteriorating. What matters more than anything else to them is the fleeting illusion of worth, of glowing like a glorious light; but they fail to see that the light is from the spontaneous combustion of their souls. Like drug addicts who sacrifice their earthly lives to the pusher for a high, men die to women. Man's wretched essence ascends to woman's soul as a love sacrifice in exchange for her glorification of him.

Beware of instant acceptance—love at first sight. You tend to believe in such love only because it sustains your

261

willfulness and rebellion against reality. In this rebellion you fall prey to illusion, and evil looks like love. Transcending this terrible ego love requires so much dedication, such a deep yearning to know and understand our ultimate purpose, that you may fall many times before the sheer pain of falling drives you to seek higher ground.

Until you find Salvation, you cannot resist love's tyranny. The conniving woman sees your efforts to hang on to some shred of common sense and reason as her mortal enemy. Deep down she knows that her man has failed her and that her loving has had something to do with the failure of both of them. She loathes having to love. All she wants to do now is punish and hurt the man for having fed his life to her ego and making it ugly and wicked.

Whatever it is, wherever it comes from (above or below), love is the mysterious ingredient that a soul needs to be complete—a complete fool or a noble being. True love is leavening a baker hid in the flour. It grows and grows until it leavens the whole lump of bread, because the baker's flour recognizes the leavening agent and responds to it by allowing the spirit of yeast to come in and fill it. In the same way, your whole being must one day respond to the truth. When you identify intuitively with the truth—you can, you know—you will be filled with love and joy. It is only because the *force* is with you that you are able to open up to these words!

Because your destiny leads to truth, false love never works for you as it seems to for other people. It is simply not compatible with your deepest, truest desire. Dissatisfaction has made you search *out there*, but the truth within you keeps trying to get your full attention, saying *That's not it—it's nowhere in the world, the world is lying.*

Up to now the lie lover has had the power to make you doubt, to bring you down into his realm, to make you seek his acceptance, beg for his sustaining lies—and just as from the lie, there proceeds a form of enslaving, life-sucking love, so from the truth in your heart will spring the true life-giving force called love. This love cannot hurt, nor can it be hurt.

Before the time of true love, you may have had many loves, and you have taken their various identities into yourself, trying to mold or remold them to fit more closely your ego heart's desire. In other words, you played God, and it is precisely this desire to play God that draws male and female together. The man feels that he can complete himself through the use of the woman, while the woman feels that she can complete herself through the use of the man—and the drama that began in Paradise with the Serpent is reenacted again and again and again, all over the world.

The Serpent's guile, which the woman instinctively used to catch the man, which he pounced on so eagerly, soon becomes a burdensome part of her nature as she sees her mate grow weaker and more needful of her. The pouncing begins to pall, but until she can recognize and correct her part of the problem or until the man sees the problem and desists from his use of her, woman will continue to suffer at the hands of men and, in turn, cause them to suffer.

Most little girls, before they are badly used by some man, dream of finding a strong, loving man, just and trustworthy in all things, a man who will be truly concerned, nonusing, protective. Surely any little girl can see herself responding to such a man with true love, bearing his children, serving him faithfully, following him to the ends of the earth. But before you can show me a man who fits that description, I will show you a chicken with teeth.

Somewhere along the line our little girl, too, gets caught up with the lure of romance as promoted by the movies and magazines. She finds herself drawn to the flawed ones. Most women simply cannot resist the appeal of the fallen man's wounded ego, the silent cry that wakens her maternal instincts and builds up her ego. In this romantic arrangement, she gets the catbird seat.

Somewhere along the line, we should be able to discover the truth of just about anything—if not through wisdom, then through experience. But some people seem determined not to learn from experience. To them, understanding never comes. They marry for the wrong reason and, thus, evolve a living hell in which the less physically powerful partner, the woman, uses the time-honored principle of seduction she acquired from the Serpent. By encouraging and slyly yielding to the part of man that is rebellious to God, she gradually transfers his loyalty to herself or, it would be more accurate to say, to the principality she represents consciously or unconsciously, willingly or unwillingly.

When you humble yourself in the service of another person's weakness, agreeing with him in all things and building up his ego, it's only a matter of time until he becomes so dependent on you, the servant, that you emerge as the master with the right to make demands on the creature you have weakened through your service. But to conquer by this technique, you must be very persistent; never go along with the sensible and good, only with the bad.

If the intended victim appears to be self-possessed and flawless, then you have to find some way to topple him. Needle him into a rage by deliberately misunderstanding or ignoring what he is trying to tell you; then when he is good and mad, turn around and comfort the madman he has become—lovingly, the same way a mother suckles the child—secretly intoxicating yourself with the nectar of power. This is a favorite trick of all tyrants, manipulating mothers, and cunning wives.

Instead of letting a child discover for himself that it's cold outside and then offering to help him on with his warm coat, a falsely loving mother *wills* him to put his coat on, "for his own good," causing the child to react badly as he *wills* back. Mother's frustration either overpowers the child or causes her to give in to his willfulness and let him have his way. Mommy then hugs him to soothe the madness—her own nature, actually, which she has implanted in him. This is the way in which all impatient, manipulating mothers ruin their children, putting a nature in them that will always cry to a mother for comfort and salvation instead of crying to God.

Thus the spirit of a mother sets a male child up to cry out to another woman's spirit in the form of a wife in whom the Serpent of old still lives. Men who have learned to be woman-needful in this fashion can always find a woman to answer those needs, and even though a man can sense that his use (and abuse) of women is leading to his downfall, he remains under a compulsion to look for salvation in the arms of women—and of course, there can be no real love in compulsion; so he hates them all, and he even hates himself for his needfulness.

Every wicked person knows and uses these strata-
gems. They are as innate and instinctive as truth is in the
conscience of one who loves God. Tease, fight, argue,
and irritate your adversary until he gives in. If he doesn't
give in, then give in yourself. Your loving embrace will
weaken the victim by nourishing the implanted flaw,
making it grow to crave more of your sustaining love.
This is the love-hate relationship. "Love" takes hold better when a victim is upset and confused to begin with, especially if *love* has seeded the confusion. "Love" is the
power of sweet tyranny everywhere, the seducer of indi-
viduals and of nations.

Therefore, no longer allow yourself to be intimidated,
and your trouble will be over. Your inordinate need for
love sets you up to be intimidated, to need love (acceptance, approval) more and more, while love itself becomes the source of intimidation and debilitation, causing
you to need more love to soothe the hate caused by *love*.
It's very confusing.

The forces of good and evil are waging war over your
soul; to win for good, you need wisdom. To find wisdom,
you must first repent of your selfish ego need for deception and false love.

Most of us are the sum total of our experiences, but another way of saying this is that we are burdened down and bothered by our past. Unless we learn to respond properly in the present moment, the present becomes merely an extension of that burdensome past.

Roy Masters, author of this persuasive self-help book, describes a remarkably simple technique to help us face life properly, calmly. He shows us that it is the way we respond emotionally to pressures which makes us sick and depressed.

By leading us back to our center of dignity and understanding and showing us how to apply one simple principle, Roy Masters shows us how to remain sane, poised, and tranquil under the most severe trials and tribulations.

Roy Masters has nothing less to offer you than the secret of life itself—how to get close to yourself and find your lost identity, the true self you have lost in the confusion.

The observation exercise materials consist of the book *How Your Mind Can Keep You Well* and three (3) cassettes of the same title. We suggest a donation of $25 or whatever you can afford.

Other Books Available
from the Foundation of Human Understanding
8780 Venice Blvd., P.O. Box 34036, Los Angeles, Ca. 90034

HOW TO CONTROL YOUR EMOTIONS
Simple instructions by which anyone may learn how to eliminate guilt, anxiety, pain, and suffering from his life forever, completely and without effort. 325 pages

HOW TO CONQUER SUFFERING WITHOUT DOCTORS
The relationship that now exists between you and your healer is the relationship which should exist within yourself. This book shows the seeker how to look inside himself for common sense and answers that are meaningful and permanent. 222 pages

SEX, SIN & SALVATION
This work explains how man's failing ego expresses itself in terms of sex and violence and how husband and wife can eventually transcend their sexual problems. 321 pages

SECRET OF LIFE
A philosophical guide to the whole riddle of existence. 194 pages

NO ONE HAS TO DIE!
There lives in this world an insidious evil force that understands and caters to our weakness, and we are delivered into the hands of the evil shepherd, and he is the author of our suffering or tragedy until we find the truth that makes us free. 243 pages

THE SATAN PRINCIPLE
The entire thrust of this book is to bring all the subtle causes of your problems into the spotlight of your consciousness. 261 pages

HOW TO SURVIVE YOUR PARENTS
Since all parents were once children, the question arises: How can we survive our parents; how do our children survive us? In no uncertain terms, this book tells how. 182 pages

All books quality paperback, $7.50 each.

MATERIALS

LECTURES BY ROY MASTERS

MEDITATION

Basics of Meditation (#1160) 90 min./$10
The Key to Meditation (#1961) 90 min./$10
Advanced Techniques of Meditation (#1176) 90 min./$10
Is Meditation for Christians? (#1944 1&2) 120 min./$12

EMOTIONAL PROBLEMS

Understanding Emotions (#1240) 90 min./$10
Emotional Blocks (#1888) 90 min./$10
The Secrets of Dealing With Stress (#2196) 90 min./$10
Happiness (#1883) 90 min./$10
Bad Habits (#1375) 90 min./$10
Psychic Vampirism (#1705) 90 min./$10
The Truth About Sex (#2112) 90 min./$10
Sex & Violence/Love & Hate (#1188) 90 min./$10
Addiction to Drugs, Sex & Alcohol (#1962) 90 min./$10
The Dangers of Music (#2195) David Masters 90 min./$10
Dominance & Subservience (#2048) 60 min./$10
Identity—Uncovering the True Self (#1960) 90 min./$10
Conquering the Suggestive Power of Words (#1500 1&2) 180 min./$20
Secrets of Salvation (#1270) 90 min./$10
Marriage: It Doesn't Have to Be a Living Hell (#2315) 90 min./$10
Bigotry (#2369) 90 min./$10
Selfishness (#2397) 90 min./$10
Change Your Attitude—Change Your Destiny (#2629) 2 tapes/$12
Dealing With Wicked Authority (#2631) 90 min./$10
A Deeper Look Into Family Problems (#2557) 90 min./$10
Becoming Perfect (#2767) 90 min./$10
The Blessings and Benefits of a Poor Memory (#2822) 90 min./$10
Revenge and Forgiveness (#2823) 90 min./$12
You Don't Have to Be Ruled by Inferior Beings (#2929) 90 min./$10
Resolving Past Sins (#2939) 90 min./$10
Seeking the Blessed State of Mind (#2975) 90 min./$10

HEALTH

Healing (#1682) 90 min./$10
Faith Healing (#2030 1&2) 130 min./$12
Faith & Hope (#1875) 90 min./$10
Sickness & Disease (#1220) 90 min./$10
Cancer & Heart Attacks (#1602) 90 min./$10
Death & Dying/Life & Living (#1112-1113) 120 min./$12
Food, Damnation & Salvation (#2835) 2 tapes, 90 min. ea./$20

RELIGION

Finding God (#2140) 60 min./$10
Be Still & Know (#1601 1&2) 120 min./$12
Beyond Knowlege (#1510 1&2) 180 min./$20
Secret Path to the Paradise State (#1116 1&2) 120 min./$12
Evolution vs. Creation (#2252) 90 min./$10
Overcoming Evil (#2256) 90 min./$10
What It Really Means to Conquer Evil (#2452) 90 min./$10
The Crisis of Faith & Doubt (#2633) 90 min./$10

SUCCESS & SURVIVAL

Moral & Financial Survival (#2131) 60 min./$10
Success w/o Ambition (#1921) 90 min./$10
Success w/o Destruction (#1922) 90 min./$10

SPECIAL SEMINARS

Hypnosis of Life/Oregon '81 (#1905) 180 min./$20
Hypnosis of Life/Boston '84 (#2853) 4 tapes, 90 min. ea./$36
Hypnosis of Life/San Francisco '85 (#2948) 4 tapes, 90 min. ea./$36

MEDITATION PACKAGE

How Your Mind Can Keep You Well
Instruction in the basic technique of meditation as taught by Roy Masters. The complete set consists of three compact cassettes and a book by the same name. $25

The basic book included in the Meditation Package above may also be obtained separately. $7.50

If you cannot afford the price of the basic meditation materials, it is the policy of the Foundation to allow you to pay what you can afford. Please be fair.

TAPE OF THE MONTH

Every month we offer a collection of the best radio conversations with Roy Masters. Each ninety-minute cassette is edited from over forty hours of live radio, to showcase the most interesting and enlightening segments of each month's broadcasts.

You can receive a full year's subscription (12 cassettes) by sending $100 for third class/$112 for first class, or you may order individual tapes by sending $10 and identifying the tape you want by month. Send subscription requests or individual tape orders to: "Tape of the Month Club," c/o The Foundation of Human Understanding.

ROY MASTERS SPEAKS

Man-Woman Relations (#1371) 60 min./$10
Man-Woman Relations, Part 2 (#1786) 90 min./$10
Man-Woman Relations, Part 3 (#1840) 90 min./$10
Man-Woman Relations, Part 4 (#2615) 90 min./$10 (Formerly 2/84 T.O.M.)
Man-Woman Relations, Part 5 (#2807) 90 min./$10 (Formerly 11/84 T.O.M.)
Resolving Family Problems (#1388) 90 min./$10
The Power of Words (#1399) 90 min./$10
Why Children Have Problems (#1410) 90 min./$10
Injustice (#1413) 90 min./$10
Dealing Properly With Children (#1441) 90 min./$10
The Effects of Music (#1525) 90 min./$10
The Meaning of Faith (#1599) 90 min./$10
False Belief (#1605) 90 min./$10
The Power of Realization (#1608) 90 min./$10
Understanding the Lower Self (#1699) 90 min./$10
Pride, the Cause of Death (#1750) 90 min./$10
All About Judgment (#2351) 90 min./$10
So You Don't Think There's a Devil, Eh? (#2423) 65 min./$10
Homosexuality: The Cause (#2443) 90 min./$10
Overcoming Overeating (#2464) 90 min./$10
Tyrants & Wimps (#2596) 90 min./$10 (Formerly Jan. T.O.M.)
Willfulness (#2665) 90 min./$10 (Formerly April T.O.M.)
Understanding Failure—The Key to Success (#2699) 90 min.$10 (Formerly May T.O.M.)
Confusing Women—Confounded Men (#2719) 90 min./$10 (Formerly June T.O.M.)
Friends, Family & Speaking Up (#2737) 90 min./$10 (Formerly August T.O.M.)
Vanity (#2817) 90 min./$10 (Formerly Nov. T.O.M.)
Doubt, Insecurity and Starting Your Own Business (#2903) 90 min./$10 (Formerly 2/85 T.O.M.)
Guiding Children With Common Sense (#2947) 90 min./$10 (Formerly 3/85 T.O.M.)
How to Give Up Smoking (#2991) 90 min./$10 (Formerly 5/85 T.O.M.)
Male Sexuality (#2993) 2 tapes, 90 min./$20
Female Sexuality (#2995) 2 tapes, 90 min./$20

POSTAGE CHART

	1 CASSETTE	1 BOOK	1 BOOK 3 CASSETTES
LIBRARY RATE	1.30	1.30	1.30
U.S. FIRST CLASS	1.75	2.75	3.75
CANADA	1.75	2.75	3.75
OVERSEAS SURFACE RATE	1.75	2.25	2.75
EUROPEAN AIR	4.00	6.00	7.25
OTHER OVERSEAS AIR	5.00	7.50	9.00